THE HIDDEN LIFE OF
Mary

From Conception to Coronation

Arthur X. Deegan II, PhD

The Hidden Life of Mary
From Conception to Coronation
Copyright © 2019 by Arthur X. Deegan II, PHD

All rights reserved. No part of this publication may be reproduced, distributed, or transmitted in any form or by any means, including photocopying, recording, or other electronic or mechanical methods, without the prior written permission of the publisher or author, except in the case of brief quotations embodied in critical reviews and certain other noncommercial uses permitted by copyright law.

Although every precaution has been taken to verify the accuracy of the information contained herein, the author and publisher assume no responsibility for any errors or omissions. No liability is assumed for damages that may result from the use of information contained within.

Library of Congress Control Number: 2019938177
ISBN-13: Paperback: 978-1-950073-15-3
          PDF: 978-1-950073-16-0
          ePub: 978-1-950073-17-7
          Kindle: 978-1-950073-18-4

Printed in the United States of America

GoToPublish LLC
1-888-337-1724
www.gotopublish.com
info@gotopublish.com

This short scripture study
is prayerfully dedicated
to my devoted grandchildren,
Ryan and Mariah,
the pride of my life
and the hope
of our future.

Contents

Introduction 13

Mary's Immaculate Conception 25

The Birth and Naming of Mary 34

Mary and the Annunciation 42

Mary and the Visitation 51

Mary and the Birth of Jesus 61

Mary and Trips To and From Egypt 70

The Naming and the Presentation of the Infant ... 76

The Holy Family in Nazareth 84

The Pilgrimage to Jerusalem 92

Mary and the Wedding at Cana 98

Mary during the Public Life of Jesus 104

Mary and the Passion and Death of Jesus 112

Mary and the Risen Christ 124

Mary and the Descent of the Spirit......................131

The Assumption of Mary 138

The Coronation of Mary as Queen 147

Foreword

At a time when Marian devotion has been on the wane, in this treasure of a spiritual meditation, Dr. Arthur Deegan offers us a fresh, scholarly, insightful, and trustworthy reflection on the hidden life of Mary, drawing upon the gospels, the church fathers, theologians, mariologists, spiritual writers, the ordinary faithful, and his own filial devotion to Our Lady.

Deegan has an uncanny ability to capture the theological and human virtues Mary evidenced in a revealing and inspirational fashion. He notes in a variety of ways that the key to Mary's privilege to be the mother of the long-awaited Messiah is her deep humility. Her selfless and unconditional surrender to God's will amidst the joys, sorrows, and inexplicable events which permeated her life enabled Mary to truly be the Mother of God and Mother of the church as well as a heroic role model for each of us to emulate.

Deegan's methodology is engaging and enjoyable to follow. He cites sixteen events recorded in the gospels or proclaimed in church doctrine (her

Immaculate Conception, Assumption into heaven, and coronation as Queen of the universe) and offers a short but excellent biblical exegesis complemented by various Marian authors and his own prayerful conversation with Mary aforementioned.

Of particular note is Mary's public interaction with Jesus. Rarely is Mary mentioned in the gospels, and even then, she often seems to be the object of a stinging rebuke. For example, when Jesus was missing in the temple for three days, upon finding him, Mary laments, "Son, why have you done this to us? Your Father and I have been looking for you with great anxiety" (Luke 2:48).

Jesus responds rather cursorily, "Did you not know I had to be about my father's business?" (Luke 2:50). The evangelist tells us, "They did not understand," and Deegan enables us to appreciate the bewilderment Mary must have experienced on that occasion.

The author's reflections upon these and other examples of the manner Mary was treated by Jesus in public resonated with me and how we, like our Blessed Lady, must learn to cope with the seemingly incomprehensible moments we encounter on our journey of discipleship.

In an age characterized by narcissism, individualism, and selfishness, Deegan relates in a very profound and practical way how Mary's life as "the handmaid of the Lord" offers us a reassuring path to holiness and caring service to others.

THE HIDDEN LIFE OF MARY

I highly recommend this well-crafted Marian journey from conception to coronation.

Most Rev. Howard J. Hubbard, Bishop Emeritus, Diocese of Albany, New York

Acknowledgments

Scripture texts in this work are taken from the *New American Bible with Revised New Testament and Psalms* © 1991, 1986, 1970, Confraternity of Christian Doctrine, Washington, DC, and are used by permission of the copyright owner. All rights reserved. No part of the New American Bible may be reproduced in any form without permission in writing from the copyright owner.

Excerpts from the Catechism of the Catholic Church, second edition, copyright 2000, Libreria Editrice Vaticana-United States Conference of Catholic Bishops, Washington, DC. Used with permission. All rights reserved.

Introduction

Why

A logical and typical question to be answered by the author of any book is: Why should we read about this topic? The first answer is so that we might emulate St. Maximilian Kolbe, whose motto was *"To love Mary and to make her loved."* More specifically about the hidden life, this term as related to Jesus and Mary often is understood to refer to those years between the presentation of the Infant in the temple to the beginning of the public life of Jesus, starting with His baptism at the Jordan River at the hand of St. John the Baptist. In other words, the period of their life when they resided quietly at Nazareth. "Hidden" because there is nothing written in sacred scripture about these thirty or so years except for the trip to Jerusalem when the Child was lost for three days.

This author would prefer to use the phrase "hidden life" to refer not to a period of time but to a characteristic of the entire life of Jesus and, for us here, of Mary. Living a hidden life is tantamount to practicing a life of perfect humility, that virtue which is called by St. Basil and many saints as the source and custodian of all the virtues. Or as St. John Chrysostom once said, "Humility is the root, mother, nurse, foundation, and bond of all virtue." Humility is said to be the prime virtue in the life of Jesus. So it was also in the life of Mary, who came closest of all humans in following the example of her Son.

Jesus said, "**Learn from me, for I am meek and humble of heart**" (Matthew 11:29), which was meant as an invitation to imitate this noble trait. In like manner, we shall approach our subject with a view toward learning from an examination of Mary's life of humility so that we can follow her example.

HOW

A second expectation of the reader at this point is some clarification as to how the material in this book will be presented. To corrupt a phrase from the gospel of St. John, there are so many books written about the Blessed Virgin Mary that soon the world will not be big enough to hold them all. In many of them, the approach taken is to study one or other event in the life or afterlife of Mary, marveling at the glory and honor which was hers as the Mother of God. These works were sometimes inspired by an apparition of Mary, calling for promotion of a particular devotion, e.g., the rosary, or dogma, e.g., the Immaculate Conception. Some few might be called actual biographies of Mary based not so much on documented historical events as on the beliefs of the faithful and the developing doctrine of Mary as directed by the official teaching of the Roman Catholic Church, sometimes called Mariology.

This is to say that despite the paucity of detailed specifics dealing with the Blessed Virgin in the gospels, there has been found, and continues to be found, a lot more about her than is often supposed. There is no direct correlation between the amount of words in scripture and the importance of a given subject.

Rarely is one single attribute of Mary examined in each important event in her life. She is discussed at various times of her life as a Sorrowful Mother or a Joyful Mother or a Queen Mother. The closest to what is proposed here can be found in chapter 5 of part 7 of the splendid book of St. John Eudes entitled *The Admirable Heart of Mary* (written in manuscript form before the French Revolution and appearing in print for the first time as part of *The Complete Works of Venerable John Eudes*, vol. VI, VII, and VIII, translated from the French in 1945). Here the author refers to the heart of Mary as an "Abyss of Humility" and enumerates twelve manifestations of Mary's marvelous humility, that is, in different episodes of her life.

Authors, from convert Edith Stein to rowing coach Erin Noelle, have told their life story in volumes entitled *The Hidden Life*. There are also books entitled The Hidden Life of Trees, Owls, Wolves, guns, cows, truffles, etc. Then there is *The Hidden Life of Freemasons* and *The Hidden Life of The Prophet*

Muhammad. Each of these focus on aspects of the chosen life which emphasize simplicity and ordinariness of lifestyle as opposed to notoriety and glamor as the source of real happiness in the life being extolled, sometimes with reference to a gift of the Creator.

The secret of Mary's ability to live a hidden life is to be found in her devotion to her Son. St. Paul referred to the Christian life as a life **"hidden with Christ in God"** (Colossians 3:3). That certainly is a summary of the life of Mary.

Such will be the attempt here: to investigate how every word or action that we know of in the life of Mary was animated above all by her virtue of humility. Lest the reader immediately recoil at the thought that Mary will be portrayed as a weak, insipid, spineless figure because of a false concept of humility, let us examine what the virtue of humility is, not as a treatise on the subject but to clarify what we shall be looking for in the life of Mary.

Humility

As with many of our philosophical concepts, we might begin by looking at the ancient Greeks, who professed a strong belief in humility. Their literature is full of examples of the harm that comes from the absence of humility; that is, the pernicious effect of hubris or pride. Often that meant thinking you were wise when you really were not. Instead, they taught, one must think of his or her abilities and talents as no greater or lesser than they really are, i.e., to be honest with oneself (cf. "The Virtuous Life," Brett and Kate McKay, blog, May 25, 2008).

Our word *humility* derives, says St. Thomas Aquinas, from the Latin *humus,* or "the earth" that lies beneath us. As applied to humans, it means that which is abject, ignoble, or in everyday language, not worth very much. As a virtue, it refers to a person considering his defects and thus having a lowly opinion of himself and willingly submitting to God and to others for God's sake. St. Bernard clarifies that by saying humility is a virtue by which a man, knowing himself as he truly is, abases himself (cf. Catholic encyclopedia on *humility*).

We must be careful not to equate humility with self-abasement alone, for such a self-image would lead to ignoring the gifts God has given us. Not showing gratitude to God for His blessings is not being humble. Christian humility, properly understood, moves on to a strong sense of self, whatever the sum of the gifts of the Creator.

Moral theologians teach that after the three theological virtues of faith, hope, and charity, there are four cardinal virtues, namely, prudence, justice, fortitude, and temperance. All other virtues are related to one or other of these. The virtue of humility is annexed to temperance, which includes all those virtues which refrain or repress the inordinate movements of our desires or appetites. Humility is thus a repressing or moderating virtue opposed to pride or vainglory (cf. Catholic encyclopedia). Humility, then, has essentially to do with the appetite, refraining from tending inordinately to greater things than is allowed by the cognitive faculty, not deeming ourselves to be above what we really are.

Benjamin Franklin is said to have written, "There is perhaps no one of our natural passions so hard to subdue as pride. Beat it down, stifle it, mortify it as much as one pleases, it is still alive. Even if I could convince myself that I had completely overcome it, I would probably be proud of my humility."

The intent here is to show Mary practiced this virtue in the highest possible degree. Several saints have expounded on how humility does admit of various degrees. For example, Ignation spirituality describes humility in terms of loving Jesus, which can be done in three ways, leading to the concept of three degrees of humility, as summarized by Fr. Joseph A. Tetlow, SJ (cf. *Making Choices in Christ*, his guide for making St. Ignatius' Spiritual Exercises, Loyola Press, Chicago, 2010).

- The first way is to love Jesus so much that nothing and no one on earth could persuade you to do what you know would cut you off from Him.
- The second way is to love Jesus so much that you want to remain loyal even to His great redemptive vision. You want to understand what Christ hopes for in the world and particularly in the church. You find real meaning in the beatitudes.
- The third way to live humility in Ignatian spirituality begins with a prayer to the Father that

He will grant you the grace to live in the way of Jesus.

Who, though he was in the form of God, did not regard equality with God something to be grasped. Rather, he emptied himself, taking the form of a slave, ... he humbled himself. (Philippians 2:6–8)

Jesus said to his disciples, **"Take care not to perform righteous deeds in order that people may see them; otherwise you will have no recompense from your heavenly father"** (Matthew 6:1). Mary lived her entire life this way. And she was not thinking of getting recompense, even from the Father. She had such a high degree of this kind of humility that her every breath was taken out of pure love for God.

St. Benedict established twelve degrees of humility (cf. *The Holy Rule of St. Benedict*, chapter 7 on "Humility"), which were defended by St. Thomas Aquinas (*Summa Theologica*, second part of part 2, question 61, answer 6). They show an increasing relationship with God going from a servile fear of God, the first degree, to a lifestyle in which a monk not only has humility in his heart but also by his very appearance so that whether he is at the work of God, in the oratory, in the monastery, in the garden, on the road, in the fields, or anywhere else, and whether sitting, walking, or standing, he should always have his head bowed and his eyes toward the ground, the twelfth degree.

Humility can also be seen as one of the virtues we practice, not only out of love of God but also out of proper love of self, i.e., as a way to attain eternal life with the Christ that we love. That was part of the teaching of Jesus when He said to His disciples, **"The greatest among you must be your servant. Whoever exalts himself will be humbled; but whoever humbles himself will be exalted"** (Matthew 23:11–12). That would seem to say that the only way to get to heaven is by being humble. St. Teresa of Avila defined humility as living in truth. While humility, like all virtues, is a gift, she warns us that we must use this gift by acts of humility or it withers and dies.

To summarize, then, the intent here is to show that Mary practiced the highest degree of the virtue of humility from conception to natural death, and even thereafter, and that she was cognizant of this, based on the words of her beautiful Magnificat, in which she sang, **"For he has looked upon his handmaid's lowliness... The Mighty One has done great things for me"** (Luke 1:48–9).

Mary thus ascribes to her humility the basis for all that God did for her. The Latin says it even better: **"Respexit Dominus humilitatem meam, et fecit in me magna, qui potent est."** Literally: "The Lord has looked upon my humility, and he who is mighty, has done great things for me." Lowliness in the English translation of Luke is simply a statement of fact and by itself amoral. But humility, the word in the Latin version of Luke, is recognizing and accepting facts, which becomes a virtue and meritorious.

We will see Mary recollected, knowing that whoever pours himself out on exterior things quickly loses the graces he has acquired. A full jewel box is always kept closed. We will see Mary avoid all those words which can draw down glory, esteem, or the appreciation of others. We will see her listen unwillingly, without interest or reflection, and with interior reluctance to the words of any, even angels, who praise or commend her. She knows it is dangerous to listen to one's own praise in the mouths of others, for that makes one lose his good judgment.

We will see Mary judge herself unworthy of any commendation. We will see Mary rejoice at hearing others praised. We will see Mary never do anything so that men may see and esteem her. She will never do anything out of human respect. She will perform all her duties perfectly because she is working in God's presence, for God and not for men. She will in every situation think more about loving than about working.

We will see Mary accept being corrected. We will see Mary willingly accept every opportunity for humbling herself. She will not be offended at a harsh word. She will welcome occasions for being disregarded and humiliated with patience, without raising any difficulties, and with joy. That will be how we will watch her perfect humility. Mary will show us how humility is the foundation of the virtues.

We will attempt to show all this by carefully following Mary in the gospels. The reader of the gospels is at first surprised to find so little about Mary; but this obscurity of Mary in the gospels has been found itself to be informative about a life of holiness, as discussed at length by many, such as Blessed Peter Canisius (de B. Virg., 1. IV, c. 24), Auguste Nicolas (La Vierge Marie d'apres l'Evangile et dans l'Eglise), Card. Newman (Letter to Dr. Pusey), and Very Rev. J. Spencer Northcote (Mary in the Gospels, London and New York, 1885, Lecture I). In the commentary on the Magnificat, published 1518, even Luther expresses the belief that the gospels praise Mary sufficiently by calling her (eight times) Mother of Jesus.

Finally, as in all attempts to extol the virtues of Mary and the consequent honor due to her, let me quickly avow that this in no way lessens the glory due to Jesus as the prime model for us to follow. As the Catechism of the Catholic Church teaches us: "What the Catholic faith believes about Mary is based on what it believes about Christ, and what it teaches about Mary illumines in turn its faith in Christ" (# 487).

========================

We will now review chronologically major phases or events in the life of Mary, seeking the lessons of humility in each of them.

THE HIDDEN LIFE OF MARY

After each discussion of an event in the life of Mary, there will be a brief conversation with Mary, in the belief that the best way to deepen a relationship with someone is through frequent one-on-one conversations, and that must be the goal we have in this study of Mary's life.

Mary's Immaculate Conception

As with all humans, Mary's life began with her conception. Scripture does not speak of this. It would appear that serious discussion about this did not begin until about the ninth century when the question of celebrating a day to honor her birth became an issue. Trying to explain St. Augustine's teaching that Mary overcame sin, some taught that he was referring only to actual sin, not original sin. Among those denying the Immaculate Conception were St. Thomas Aquinas and St. Bernard.

- Aquinas was of the opinion that maybe God rescued Mary within an instant of her conception so that, conceived in sin, she was born pure of sin.

- Bernard, even though often called "the bearer of the flame for Mary," was convinced she needed to be redeemed like all humans, so she must have had original sin. But he would accept the doctrine if pronounced by a pope.

- Duns Scotus favored her Immaculate Conception based on the theological method called maximalism which said if it is not against sacred scripture or the authority of the church, then it seems preferable to attribute greater, rather than lesser, excellence to Mary.

While theologians wrestled with the concept of her Immaculate Conception, iconographic devotions were highlighting the popular belief of the people in her privilege. Painters, sculptors, poets, and humanists all avowed their belief in it. The Council of Basel in 1439 came close to defining it as a dogma, but its decrees were declared invalid over a dispute regarding the primacy of the pope. Even the Council of Trent, a hundred years later (1545–1563), drafted a document about this honor to her but did not define it as a doctrine de fide.

It took several more centuries before the private devotion on the part of the faithful taught that Mary was not only a perpetual virgin Mother of God, but because of her destiny, she was never without the fullness of grace. As stated by the Catechism of the Catholic Church (#492), quoting Lumen Gentium, 53, 56: The "splendor of an entirely unique holiness" by which Mary is "enriched from the first instant of her conception" comes wholly from Christ: she is "redeemed, in a more exalted fashion, by reason of the merits of her Son."

Adam and Eve were also with the fullness of grace as the greatest work of God's early creation. They lived a life of joy and contentment in the Garden of Eden. We can imagine how this blessed state was pleasing to God as they guarded His creation as loyal servants of their Creator. That is, until they gave in to the blasphemous promises of a serpent that they would be like gods (cf. Genesis 3:5). The difference with Mary was that she was to crush the head of the serpent, **the most cunning of all the wild animals that God had made** (Genesis 3:1). Mary's Immaculate Conception brought with it the gift of being satisfied with her state as a beloved creature of God, never giving in to disloyal suggestions of the devil to seek higher honor than was given to her, a mark of her deep humility.

In 1830, Mary appeared to St. Catherine Laboure to ask for a medal to be struck in her honor.

The image was to be of Mary with these words around the edge "O Mary, conceived without sin, pray for us who have recourse to thee." The emphasis in these apparitions was not on Mary but on convincing people to ask for graces that would otherwise not be granted. It was not quite time for a more open avowal of Mary's immaculate condition.

Shortly thereafter, in 1854, the singular gift of Mary's Immaculate Conception was declared a dogma of the church by Pope Pius IX (cf. his Ineffabilis Deus). By this the church teaches that Mary was conceived in the womb of her mother, St. Anne, free from original sin by virtue of the foreseen merits of her son Jesus Christ (Catechism of the Catholic Church, 491–2; Vatican Council II, Lumen Gentium 53, 56).

This gift meant Mary did not have original sin. St. Augustine, with extraordinary perceptiveness, described the nature of this sin as follows: *amor sui usque ad contemptum Dei*—self-love to the point of contempt of God. It was *amor sui* which drove our first parents toward that initial rebellion and then gave rise to the spread of sin throughout human history. Mary, from the first moment of her conception, lived the opposite way: *amor Dei usque ad contemptum sui*—love for God to the point of contempt of self.

In 1858, Mary appeared to fourteen-year-old Bernadette Soubirous and identified herself as the Immaculate Conception. Ever since the local bishop officially declared that Mary had indeed appeared to Bernadette, the church has accepted the reality of the eighteen appearances of Mary at Lourdes, which attest to her deep humility.

Note to whom Mary was going to confirm this important doctrine of the Church: a poor, simple, hard-working peasant teenager. Could there be a less pretentious bearer of this good news? Mary has always seemed to favor only such humble persons with her private revelations. That has got to be not a coincidence but an attestation of Mary's own humility.

Note how Mary spoke to Bernadette. Just as an archangel spoke with submissiveness to the teenaged Mary at her Annunciation, so she in turn here almost begs Bernadette: "Would you do me the kindness of coming here for fifteen days?" Mary never demands; she assumes the role of a pleader.

Note where the apparitions took place: it was called Massabielle. At the time of Bernadette, this Grotto was a dirty, hidden, damp, and cold place. It was called the pigs' shelter because that was where the pigs feeding in the area usually took shelter. Mary had given birth to her divine Son in another animal shelter and thus once more showed her predilection for the lowly.

Note that despite the tradition from the early Church that Mary was immaculate, she herself waited until the successor of Peter proclaimed this as a dogma before she spoke about this gift to herself. To wait some eighteen centuries before speaking of it is indeed a great measure of self-control.

Note further that even though Bernadette asked Mary who she was in each of the apparitions, it was not until the seventeenth vision that Mary answered the question, which had to be asked four times in this next to last appearance of Mary to Bernadette. Before speaking about herself, Mary, in all the earlier conversations with the peasant girl, spoke about penance, about praying for sinners, about opening a spring of curative waters. Mary put the discussion of herself last as a living example of her humility.

Mary was following the practice advocated by Jesus when He told His followers that they should seat themselves at the lowest place, not the head of the table, and wait to be invited to come up higher by their host.

A Brief Conversation with Mary

Sweet mother Mary, thank you for this lesson on humility. How mollified I am to think of how often I like to talk about myself, contrary to your example here. After Adam and Eve, no human other than you entered this world in the state of grace. While aware of this singular gift of God, you chose not to speak of it until centuries of devout Christian artists and pilgrims proclaimed it from their hearts. Someone has said, "The icons of artists are to images what the scriptures of the Holy Spirit are to words—namely proof that God has visited His people and blessed His holy ones."

I try to understand that this gift of your Immaculate Conception was the work of the Holy Spirit preparing a worthy dwelling place for the Word made flesh. Some have expressed the opinion that the Spirit chose you for this special calling because of your great humility. It seems like the proverbial chicken and egg conundrum. Which came first: your humility that attracted the Holy Spirit? Or the gifts of the Spirit that taught you humility?

This gift meant you did not have original sin. St. Augustine, with extraordinary perceptiveness, described the nature of this sin as self-love to the point of contempt for God. It was love of self which drove our first parents toward that initial rebellion and then gave rise to the spread of sin throughout human history.

Daily as I recite the prayers of the novena dedicated to you under your title of Mary, conceived without sin, I am reminded that your Son has wished that no flesh may glory in His sight. He wished that your miraculous medal be manifested to St. Catherine Laboure for a better and more widely diffused belief in your Immaculate Conception. I pledge myself to promote this special devotion to honor you and also to commit myself to follow your example of a life hidden in the love of Jesus.

As I look with filial love at the reverse of your medal, I am reminded of the intimate connection between the cross and yourself, represented by the initial M. I find comfort and strength in seeing the image of your immaculate heart next to the image of the sacred heart of your Son, where I see the height to which the lowliness of your life has been acknowledged by God.

As I meditated on your being conceived without sin, I was reminded that the word *conceive* is derived from the Latin, meaning "to seize, to take hold of." Yes, God really took hold of you when you were conceived; so strongly did He seize you that you began living in the womb of St. Anne without a single blemish. Only the purest of the pure could be that close to God, and so only your Immaculate Conception was appropriate. May God take hold of me and keep me close to Him always.

God permitted you to be an exception to the rule that all humans are conceived with original sin. The reason for this gift was that you were to bear the Son of God in your womb for nine months as a living tabernacle. As I reflect on this, I am ashamed of how different is the case with me: I am privileged to receive that same Son of God in Holy Communion so that I too become a living tabernacle. But how defiled is my soul by actual sins that I have committed. Pray for me, loving mother, so that I work hard to make of myself a clean receptacle for the Bread of Life.

From the history of how difficult it was to get the magisterium to define the dogma of your Immaculate Conception, may I learn to be a proponent of all the honors being thought of for you. May I not be deterred from singing your praises for fear of displeasing others whose love for you has yet to be awakened.

As I live in a country dedicated in a special way to your Immaculate Conception, help me to praise God for His goodness to you and to us in this land of the free. O Mary, conceived without sin, pray for us who have recourse to thee.

O Mary, keep reminding me of how small I really am. Amen.

The Birth and Naming of Mary

The Church celebrates the feast of the Immaculate Conception on December 8. It is not surprising, therefore, that she fixes the feast of Mary's birth some nine months later, on September 8. Again sacred scripture does not speak of this event. What details about it that have come down through the centuries are based on an apocryphal book called the Protoevangelium of James (5:2).

This document, which was probably put into its final written form in the early second century, describes Mary's father, Joachim, as a wealthy member of one of the Twelve Tribes of Israel. He and his wife, Anne, were deeply grieved by their childlessness. It is not clear where the actual birth took place. Some accounts speak of Nazareth, and others say it was in a house near the Sheep Gate in Jerusalem. It is possible that a wealthy man such as Joachim had a home in both Judea and Galilee (cf. "Nativity of Mary," *Wikipedia, the free encyclopedia*).

Only the Blessed Virgin and St. John the Baptist are honored by feast days commemorating their birth into this world. All other saints are remembered on the anniversary of their birth into a second life in heaven. This honor is not so much to recognize them as important persons in the history of the Church but to give testimony to their important mission in cooperation with Jesus and in the life of the Church. Mary, singular descendant child of Israel, is both the most worthy representative of the people of the Old Covenant but also the hope and the dawn of the whole world. With her, after a long expectation of the promises of a Messiah, the times are fulfilled and a new economy is established (cf. Lumen Gentium, 55). The birth of Mary is important in light of her choice as Mother of the Savior. Her existence is indissolubly connected with that of Christ.

ARTHUR X. DEEGAN II, PHD

In the seventeenth century, the history of the birth and life of the Blessed Virgin Mary was revealed to Venerable Mary of Jesus of Agreda. In apparitions of Mary to this holy nun, the latter was instructed to write it all down. That became a four-volume, 2,676-page work entitled *The Mystical City of God*, reputed by its ardent supporters as perhaps the most important book every written, second only to the Bible (cf. *The Mystical City of God* by Venerable Mary of Jesus of Agreda, 1602–1665, whose body remains incorrupt to this day). In it we are told

- that Mary possessed the moral and natural virtues in a supernatural manner;
- that she was full of the gifts and grace of the Holy Spirit as no other human was;
- that she was conversant with the whole natural and supernatural order of things.
- that from the first instant of her life in the womb of her mother she was wiser, more prudent, more enlightened, and more capable of comprehending what was required of His creatures than all the creatures that ever existed, excepting of course her most holy Son.

In keeping with the thesis that Mary's humility was present in every action and phase of her life, let us reflect on the name given to our Blessed Mother at her birth. What does the name of Mary signify? St. Jerome saw the etymology for this name to be "a drop of water from the sea (stilla maris)." Is there anything more insignificant than a drop in the bucket? Maybe it could be a drop in the ocean. So from her very christening, Mary is spoken of as amounting to next to nothing. This sounds like the epitome of humility expressed by many of the saints when they professed to the Lord that they are worth nothing of themselves.

St. Bernard of Clairvaux taught that if the winds of temptations surge, if you run aground on the shoals of troubles, look to this star, call upon Mary! If you are tossed by the winds of pride or ambition or detraction or jealousy, look to this star, call upon Mary! If anger or greed or the allurements of the flesh dash against the boat of our mind, look to Mary (Magnificat, September 2009, p. 158).

Richard of St. Laurence proclaimed that there is not such powerful help in any name, nor is there any other name given to men, after that of Jesus, from which so much salvation is poured forth upon men as from the name of Mary. He rejoiced that the devout invocation of this sweet and holy name leads to the acquisition of superabundant graces in this life and a very high degree of glory in the next. St. Alphonsus of Liguori (+1787) founder of the Redemptorists, encouraged sinners to have recourse to this great name because it alone will suffice to cure them of all their evils, and there is no disorder, however malignant, that does not immediately yield to the power of the name of Mary (Magnificat, September 2007, p. 157–158).

Blessed Raymond Jordano preached that however hardened and diffident a heart may be, the name of this most Blessed Virgin has such efficacy that if it is only pronounced, that heart will be wonderfully softened.

St. Methodius prayed, "Your name, O mother of God, is filled with divine graces and blessings." So much so that St. Bonaventure declares "that your name, O Mary, cannot be pronounced without bringing some grace to him who does so devoutly."

But now note that the name Mary was not totally self-effacing. When Isidore of Seville considered the name of Mary *stilla*, meaning drop, it was morphed somehow to *stella* or star of the sea, which became one of Mary's most popular appellations from the ninth century on with the writing of the beloved hymn "Ave Maris Stella." Ironically, this one-word change presented an entirely different characteristic of Mary. Because the star of the sea was held up as a source of courage, this symbol now saw her as the lodestar of voyagers, protecting them from enemies and storms to a safe haven until the end of their journey.

Tradition held that the child of Anne and Joachim followed the Jewish customs of the time for young girls, including years of service in the temple. Throughout the centuries, poets and painters have delighted in depicting the innocent girl comporting herself in a simple, pure, and joyful manner. They seem to have fixated on her living an innocent and humble lifestyle.

A Brief Conversation with Mary

Sweet mother Mary, thank you for this lesson on humility. I applaud the generosity of our heavenly Father in gifting you so richly with all the virtues I too am called upon to practice, especially the virtue of humility seen in your very name, Mary. I have no misconceptions about the work it will take on my part to be worthy of being one of your beloved children. I know the insidious ways that my self-interest creeps into my every thought and action. I humbly beg your patience in overlooking my pride and pray earnestly to follow you, Star of the Sea.

For generations, Mary has been among the most popular names parents give to their daughters. I am sure that their intention was to afford the girls a patron to follow who would show them how to live pure, humble lives. How many women do I know who bear that same lovely name. My own mother and sister are among them. What lessons of humility these ladies have been for me. It must not be pure coincidence that I do not know anyone with that name who besmirched it. Simplicity, cooperation, and forgiveness mark their way of life. Thank you for these models of behavior.

Every knee must bend and every head must bow at the mention of the holy name of Jesus. Your own blessed name is deserving of similar respect, in acknowledgement of your cooperation with Jesus in winning our salvation, and as a sign of honor due you in that regard. With St. Peter Canisius, I am convinced that there is no other name more glorious or powerful than your holy name (Magnificat, September 2014, p. 159–160). As Blessed Henry Suso exclaimed, "O Mary, what must you yourself be, since your name is so beautiful?" Even on a purely human way of thinking, why should we not bend the knee before you who had fourteen kings in your ancestry?

By keeping your name on my lips, I show my devotion to you. When I repeat your name, I greatly honor God, your Creator. You never kept any glory for yourself. Your soul magnifies the Lord (cf. Luke 1:46). To you we can attribute the verse in Song of Songs 1:3, "**Your name spoken is a spreading perfume —.**"

How often I call on you by name, after the example of the heavenly messenger, Gabriel, especially in reciting your holy rosary. Twice in each Hail Mary, recited fifty-three times in each of the four groups of mysteries, do I speak your lovely name. St. Louis de Montfort avers that praying the Hail Mary will cause the Word of God to take root in my soul and bring forth Jesus, the fruit of life, just as it did in your womb. Help me to be less distracted as I recite that name, for it calls to mind the kind of life I should be leading. By myself I am less than a drop in the bucket; though as one of your devoted legionnaires,

THE HIDDEN LIFE OF MARY

I can help point others to your guiding light. Hail Mary, blessed art thou.

O Mary, keep reminding me of how small I really am. Amen.

Mary and the Annunciation

What is sometimes called the first moment of Catholic salvation history was the occasion of the Annunciation to the Blessed Virgin that she was to be the Mother of God. There are three discernible mental states on the part of Mary during the visit of

Gabriel, the messenger of God, as recounted by St. Luke (Luke 1:26–38).

First we are told of the greeting made by the angel. Gabriel does not say "Shalom," or "Peace be with you," the usual Jewish greeting. Instead he says "Hail." The deeper meaning of the Greek word used by Luke is "rejoice." The same word is used by the angel to the shepherds in Bethlehem: "**Do not be afraid, for behold, I proclaim to you good news of great joy that will be for all the people**" (Luke 2:10). So we take this word and make it the first word of our Hail Mary, which is a prayer of great joy. In Latin, the word is *Ave*. The Romans used that word in a specific way. Their salutation, as in "Hail, Caesar," was a mark of respect and politeness, even subservience. Imagine that: one of the seven archangels being respectful and polite to a little teenaged girl! Several noted artists, in painting this scene, have Gabriel actually kneeling before Mary (e.g., Orazio Gentileschi, "Annunciation," c. 1623, in the Galleria Sabauda, Turin).

But that was not Mary's self-image. Luke says her first reaction was to be troubled and to wonder what kind of greeting this could be. So obviously troubled was she that Gabriel immediately told her, "**Do not be afraid, Mary, for you have found favor with God**" (Luke 1:30). There are some who say Mary, during her formative years assisting in the temple, was no stranger to visions or visits of angels (cf. "Our Lady was accustomed to visits from angels," St. Thomas, *Summa Theologica*, III, Q 30, a.3 ad 3), but we have no corroboration of that. We must assume, then, that this visit from Gabriel was truly troubling to her, given her simple humility. *How can it be that I am greeted with such politeness by an angel?* thought Mary. She was fearful, or disconcerted, because her true knowledge of her own station in life did not allow for angels being subservient to her.

Then Gabriel makes clear who was to carry out the age-old promise to David when he says, "**You will conceive in your womb and bear a son, and you shall name him Jesus. He will be great and will be called Son of the Most High, and the Lord God will give him the throne of David his father, and he will rule over the house of Jacob forever, and of his kingdom there will be no end**" (Luke 1:30–33).

This prompted a second reaction on the part of Mary. In keeping with her self-image of being unworthy, she asks, "**How can this be, since I have no relations with a man?**" (Luke 1:34). She could have said, in keeping with her simple state in life, "You cannot mean that such an honor is being given to me, a humble servant of the Lord!" As a nubile Jewish maiden, Mary must have thought about having a child. But she had no ambitious visions of she or her child being special in the eyes of God. So she needed to get this clarified.

Earlier, Zechariah, a revered Jewish priest of the temple, doubted the word of the angel announcing the coming birth of his son, John the Baptist, for which he was struck mute. Mary, a simple teenager, did not doubt; she asked for clarification. She could have insisted that she was not worthy of what had just been told to her. Instead, her unwillingness to argue with a messenger from God made her state a reason for an explanation—that she had "**no relations with a man**" (Luke 1:34) despite being betrothed to Joseph. A very natural way for a simple Jewish girl to feel. St. Augustine explains that she had already taken a vow of virginity and the betrothal was to protect that vow. She is no longer locked in her troubled state; now she seeks to understand. She simply wants to know what is expected of her. Immediately, her humility leads her to accept whatever strange future is predicted by the angel, even if far above her station in life.

The angel obliges by giving her all the details she needs to know. **"The holy Spirit will come upon you, and the power of the Most High will overshadow you. Therefore the child to be born will be called holy, the Son of God"** (Luke 1:35). Mary may become the Mother of God, but at the moment, she is still a simple Jewish maiden. At these words of Gabriel, she is still taken aback because of her true humility and may have stared blankly at the angel. Her mind is trying to catch up with her desire to obey. To dispel any possible lingering confusion, Gabriel is quick to add, **"And behold, Elizabeth, your relative, has also conceived a son in her old age, and this is the sixth month for her who was called barren; for nothing will be impossible for God"** (Luke 1:36–37).

Gabriel's rather long answer to Mary's question shows the care God is taking, through his messenger, to calmly and quietly lead this simple girl to an understanding of what she is being asked to do while leaving her reply to be totally voluntary. Mary is not being asked to submit her will without some understanding of what is entailed. And so as to dispel in Mary's simple mind any doubt that such a thing could happen, Gabriel added the news about Elizabeth. Happy news—yes. But presented as a reminder that God could make happen even the most unthinkable events.

At that comes Mary's third reaction. **"Behold, I am the handmaid of the Lord. May it be done to me according to your word"** (Luke 1:38). The term "handmaid" is very much in keeping with the thought expressed earlier that Mary was the servant of the Lord. As such, she can do nothing but agree to what was being asked of her. On the other hand, she does seem to realize that this was not a command: she was being asked for her consent.

Servants are always in a position of carrying out the master's wishes either happily and willingly or halfheartedly if not outright disdainfully. Mary's humility saw the need for some kind of an answer. Being truly in the service of her Lord, she chose to give her consent by carefully choosing words that would indicate what her third state of mind was at that point. So when she chose the word *handmaid*, she was describing her consent as freely given, totally acceptable, and with her complete endorsement.

St. Bernard of Clairvaux sees great drama here. After the error of our first parents, the world was dark. God wanted to restore friendship with mankind. He wants to enter the world anew. He knocks on Mary's door. He needs human free will to say yes to counter Adam and Eve's no. God created free will; His power is dependent on the unforceable consent of humans. Heaven and earth is holding its breath at this moment. Will Mary say yes? Or will her humility hold her back? Just this once, Bernard wants her not to be humble but daring by saying yes. And she did (cf. *Jesus of Nazareth—the Infancy Narratives* by Pope Benedict XVI, Image Press, NY, 2012, p. 36).

Is that contrary to her characteristic of humility? Certainly not. The truly humble person who has chosen to live his or her life in consort with the will of the Father recognizes what the will of God is. Mary humbly concurs so that her will continues to be one with that of her God. Her saying in effect "Thy will be done" was the same prayer later taught by Jesus Himself as part of the Our Father: "Thy will be done."

Zechariah had doubted because his message was about an exception to human natural events, namely the age at which women could conceive. Mary's message was about turning upside down the human-God relationship, namely a human carrying God in her womb, a much more unbelievable message. Yet Mary accepted and believed because of the total subservience of her understanding and will to the will of God.

Here we see how her humility feeds and strengthens her faith, a theological virtue.

Mary's humility was not one of passivity. She was not subservient to the point of blindly carrying out what were presented as orders. Her role as servant of the Lord, *doule kyriou* in Greek, was the feminine version of *doulas Jesou Christou*, slave of Jesus Christ, which was the description of the Apostles of the Lord as they carried out His orders. They certainly did not live a life of passivity. They were active, even aggressive in carrying out their mission. The same has been the case with the pontiffs starting with Gregory the Great, who was the first to call himself *servus servorum Dei*. Jaroslav Pelican devotes a chapter to showing how Mary the Handmaid has always also been considered the Woman of Valor through the ages. (The handmaid of the Lord becomes the Woman of Valor, cf. detail by Jaroslav Pelican in his documented study of *Mary Through the Centuries*, Yale University Press, New Haven, CT, 1923, chapter 6.)

Mary thus became the mother of God. **"Then the angel departed from her,"** (Luke 1:38) for his work was done. Now it was all up to Mary. From being understandably troubled, to being carefully inquisitive, to giving an unconditional yes, Mary begins an entirely new life, one of intimate relations with her Creator-Son, now in her womb; one of peace and joy and humbly carrying out the will of the Father.

A Brief Conversation with Mary

Sweet mother Mary, thank you for this lesson on humility. From your conversation with Gabriel, you were made aware of the plan of God concerning His Son. You were the first of those "little ones" of whom Jesus will one day say: **"Father ... although you have hidden these things from the wise and the learned, you have revealed them to the childlike"** (Matthew 11:25).

Help me to imitate your simplicity so that I may understand more of God's plan, at least as it affects me. In desiring to submit my will to that of our Father, I cannot rely on a message from an angel. But I can subject my pride to a careful consideration of how you readily and freely accepted the mission put before you by the archangel. I pray for the stamina to overcome my pride in bowing to the role I am called upon to follow.

You were faced with the challenge of humbly accepting the truth of the most unbelievable story ever told to a human, and you did not hesitate to give it your assent. Help me, I pray, to remember that the Annunciation to you is more importantly the Incarnation of Jesus and to realize that this miraculous event is one of the cornerstones of my pitiable faith.

In contemplating this most admirable event in your early life, may I never forget that this is when you became the Mother of God, your most important title. By humbly agreeing to the message of the angel, you rose to a height above all men and angels. You became the Ark of the Covenant, another title of yours which emphasizes your privilege in becoming the tent of God, the realization of what all cultures throughout history naturally sought, namely, that God would dwell among us.

This event was really your discerning your vocation in life, something we all have to do sooner or later and sometimes more than once. One might scoffingly say that you had the benefit of an archangel to help you know what the will of God was for you, a luxury we do not have. But the reality is that we receive messages from God in numerous ways. We pray to be inspired by the Holy Spirit in figuring out what our life's work should be.

I remember reading how an elderly and handicapped person was kept awake nights trying to discern what God wanted him to do with his remaining months or years since he was past the prime of his life. He wrote that it came to him as he lay looking at his wife sleeping next to him that the will of the Father for him was simply to take care of her and to love their children and their neighbors.

O Mary, mother and model of all vocations, assist us in determining what it is that the Lord wishes from us. Help us to be as generous as you were in giving your unconditional yes.

O Mary, keep reminding me of how small I really am. Amen.

Mary and the Visitation

With Gabriel's departure, Mary is a different person—she is now the Mother of God. She begins this new life not thinking about herself but remembering the message about Elizabeth being with child.

During those days Mary set out and traveled to the hill country in haste to a town of Judah (Luke 1:39).

Why the haste? Spiritual writers have offered three reasons. First, she is now in possession of news that the Jewish people have been awaiting for centuries: the Messiah has come. She is anxious to share the unbelievable, wonderful news. As the first living tabernacle, carrying the second person of the Blessed Trinity within her, Mary did not hesitate to be the first bearer of the Good News even to one who herself was blessed by a special miracle of conception. Mary's humility made her anxious to share what she knew and not keep this gem to herself. She would not be bragging about it but exultingly sharing it.

A second reason evinced by some for Mary's hasty visit concerns a very possible initial desire on the part of Mary when she heard the surprising news that her elder cousin Elizabeth was with child. Rather than doubt such an unusual event, as Zechariah had done, we can envision Mary's young and excitable mind thinking, *Wow! What wonderful news! I've got to see this!* And with that, she rushes off to witness this happy revelation. Such a reaction shows Mary's humility again, not only because she accepted the angel's word at face value but also because such a sudden inspiration to go and see for herself is consistent with not trusting her own ears and wanting verification.

The third reason for Mary's quick decision to go to her cousin was the desire to be of assistance to the older woman. Mary understood that Gabriel's mention of Elizabeth's pregnancy was a suggestion that Mary think not of herself but of someone in need of assistance. We are told by St. Luke (1:56) that Mary stayed three months with Elizabeth. Since the latter had been pregnant for six months when Gabriel made his announcement to Mary, the inference is that Mary stayed to assist in whatever way she could until the birth of John, after which she would no longer be needed. Every act she performed to ease the unusual birthing time for Elizabeth was another act of humble service.

In El Grego's famous oil painting of the *Visitation*, the painter has drawn two women of about the same size and attire facing each other on an equal footing. He is showing Mary's humble response to her cousin's initial wonder at being visited by the mother of her Lord. Elizabeth wanted to make Mary the important person here, the one to be served. But Mary would have none of it. She is shown touching her elder relative lovingly to indicate that she came to serve and not to be served, a clear mark of her great humility.

Looking carefully at how St. Luke reported this visitation, we can see in every verse of his gospel how Mary's humility animated her being.

Mary enters the house of Zechariah and greets Elizabeth (Luke 1:40). We don't know what words she used to greet her cousin, but doubtless they were an expression of joy, congratulating Elizabeth on her good fortune. She must have intended to let her cousin know that she was here to be of assistance. But Elizabeth immediately turned the attention away from herself and back to Mary. **"When Elizabeth heard Mary's greeting, the infant leaped in her womb, and Elizabeth, filled with the holy Sprit, cried out in a loud voice and said, "Most blessed are you among women, and blessed is the fruit of your womb."** (Luke 1:41–42).

Elizabeth experiences a quick movement of the child in her womb and, being filled with the Holy Spirit, realizes this is no ordinary fetus movement. Her child was recognizing the presence of Him for whom he would eventually be preparing the way. Elizabeth too recognized the presence of her Lord in the womb of Mary and calls the teenager blessed precisely because she carried the most blessed child as fruit of her womb.

"And how does this happen me, that the mother of my Lord should come to me? For at the moment the sound of your greeting reached my ears, the infant in my womb leaped for joy. Blessed are you who believed that what was spoken to you by the Lord would be fulfilled" (Luke 1:43–45).

Here Elizabeth explains that Mary is blessed because she accepted the words of Gabriel and believed that what he foretold would take place. We can readily imagine that Elizabeth recalled what had happened to her husband because he did not accept the message of the angel to him. We hear nothing during this visitation from Zechariah because he is to remain mute until the christening of his son.

Mary was coming to Elizabeth to share her good news. But her cousin already knew what had happened. And most importantly for proper understanding of the development of the doctrine of Mary, she knew why it had happened, namely, because Mary believed the message of the angel (cf. Pope John Paul 11, Encyclical letter, *Mother of the Redeemer (Redemptoris Mater)*, March 25, 1987, 12).

What flattery indeed is this effusive greeting from Elizabeth. She is being told by her much older cousin that she is one in a million, so to speak, blessed among all women. As indeed she was. But Mary is not going to let this praise go unexplained. Her rejoinder comes from her own proper understanding of what had taken place, of who deserves to be the focus of attention.

> **"My soul proclaims the greatness of the Lord; my spirit rejoices in God my savior. For he has looked upon his handmaid's lowliness; behold, from now on will all ages call me blessed."**
> (Luke 1:46–48)

To paraphrase: "Instead of dwelling on my being so fortunate," says Mary, "let's recognize that despite my little worth, God wishes me to give Him the glory. And if I am to be called blessed throughout the ages, it is because God has recognized my unworthiness and is using my humble submission to His will as a reason for all to praise Him." Mary proclaims or praises aloud that "God is great." Long before followers of Allah made this simple phrase a battle cry, Mary accepts the acknowledgment of her cousin that she has received many gifts. But the point is that she recognizes and proclaims that they are gifts, not anything she has merited on her own: the essence of humility.

> **"The Mighty One has done great things for me, and holy is his name."** (Luke 1:49)

Clearly Mary is saying that she does not deserve any credit or honor; it is the Almighty who has made all this happen and who is to be recognized as deserving of praise.

> **"His mercy is from age to age to those who fear him."** (Luke 1:50)

Mary wants to remind Elizabeth that what God has done for and to her is not without precedent. Without going into any one-to-one comparison, for she certainly acknowledges that her situation is without parallel, she points out that through the centuries God has been merciful to anyone who fears, that is, obeys, Him. She is trying to move the attention away from her and to the Lord who is behind all this.

> **"He has shown might with his arm, dispersed the arrogant of mind and heart. He has thrown down the rulers from their thrones but lifted up the lowly. The hungry he has filled with**

good things; the rich he has sent away empty. He has helped Israel, his servant, remembering his mercy, according to his promise to our fathers, to Abraham and to his descendants forever." (Luke 1:51–55)

These verses are reflections on the Old Testament, showing how comfortable Mary was with the words of scripture. She lived these words herself; they animated her life. She here sublimates her gifts to the greatness of God and His manner of dealing with humans, with which she was very familiar. She also prefigures the teaching of Jesus in the beatitudes.

This wonderful hymn of Mary mirrors her entire being. The entire personality of Mary is shown in this word portrait of her soul. Mary magnifies—that is, proclaims—the greatness of the Lord. It is a wonderful hymn of praise at any time, but when sung at this moment, when Elizabeth is trying to praise Mary, this can be seen as a manifestation of the constant readiness of Mary to remove attention from herself.

A Brief Conversation with Mary

Sweetest mother Mary, thank you for this lesson on humility. How eagerly you put aside the honor shown you in becoming the Mother of God in favor of coming to the aid of your older cousin. Help me to be less eager for the esteem of others. Help me to shun being in the spotlight. Help me to imitate your humility. May I accept whatever graces the Lord gives me but be quick to use them to give Him the praise and honor.

It was clear in your words to Elizabeth that while you and she were the subject of much attention because of your pregnancies, it was still Jesus who was center stage. He caused John to leap in his mother's womb; He was the one you praised as the cause of the adulation you would receive. May I also remember who it is who deserves praise for any good that I might do.

Your visit to Elizabeth was born of a desire to be of aid to her. Please help me to take advantage of every opportunity that presents itself to be of aid to others in need.

Help me to love Jesus as you did and to bring Him to others as you did. I can do this by being an extraordinary minister of the Blessed Sacrament. I can do this by joining with others in faith sharing groups and Bible study groups. I acknowledge the need to make Him great in my life, rather than basking in my good fortune.

I think of the present-day emphasis in the church on evangelization. Certainly important to Jesus when He sent His followers to baptize all nations but not stressed as much as it should be in recent decades. You, in your haste to bring the news of the Messiah to Elizabeth, are a prime example of evangelizing. As I contemplate your visitation, I think of all those who would have us believe there is no need for what they call religion. They would have us believe we waste untold fortunes by building churches and supporting preachers and supporting programs of evangelization. If only they would meditate on the parables of your Son teaching us not to hide our light under a bushel. We need organized religion to carry out the command to bring the good news to all, as you did to Elizabeth. Thank you for the example to follow.

Elizabeth's description of you is noteworthy. She called you blessed because you believed. She called you a woman of faith. Had you not believed, you could not have given your unconditional yes. Help me to be blessed as one of **those who have not seen and have believed** (John 20:29). I realize that my faith must not be primarily a set of formulas or creed that I memorize and recite. Neither is my faith to be an abstract virtue that can be neatly defined. No, it must be a personal, mysterious encounter with the living God, with Jesus Christ. May I be blessed to enjoy an intimate personal relationship with your Son, trying to imitate your humility as the demeanor that He might find attractive in me.

You took pains to say in your Magnificat that all that was taking place with you and Elizabeth was attributed to the mercy of God, which was consistent with His attitude toward humans down through the ages. The name of God is mercy according to both Pope Benedict XVI and Pope Francis. It was His mercy that prompted Him to work the wonder of your pregnancy. It was His mercy that had decided "the fullness of time" had come, and it was through you that the Messiah was finally to redeem humankind. The uniqueness of your selection for this, attested to by Elizabeth did not give you a swelled head. Rather it elicited from you this hymn of humble witness to the glory and goodness of God.

O Mary, keep reminding me of how small I really am. Amen.

Mary and the Birth of Jesus

After the visitation, Mary is found at home in Nazareth and suddenly betrothed to a man named Joseph without any explanation as to how this occurred. There are apocryphal legends about this, but nothing supported by scripture or recognized by history. Nonetheless, even in one such legend, we can see how Mary is already a handmaid.

According to this story, when she was fourteen, the high priest wished to send her home for marriage. Mary reminded him of her vow of virginity, and in his embarrassment, the high priest consulted the Lord. Then he called all the young men of the family of David and promised Mary in marriage to him whose rod should sprout and become the resting place of the Holy Ghost in form of a dove. It was Joseph who was privileged in this extraordinary way. Thus Mary accepted what others said was the will of God. Several of the early fathers of the church, like St. Gregory of Nyssa, St. Germain of Constant, and pseudo-Gregory Nazianzen seem to adopt such a legend, perhaps specifically to point out this submission on the part of Mary.

Mary returned to Nazareth and her betrothed Joseph to complete the time of her pregnancy. But apparently, Mary's condition was not at first known to Joseph. **"When his mother Mary was betrothed to Joseph, but before they lived together, she was found with child through the holy Spirit"**. (Mt. 1:18). Being a righteous man, Joseph intended to divorce Mary quietly so as not to shame her. We can imagine the sorrow that caused Mary. Here she was, the favored one of God to be chosen to be His mother; here she was, to be called blessed by all ages because of the gift given to her. And now her fiancé intends to dishonor her, even though quietly, and leave her to give birth in shame. Maybe a divorce could be kept quiet but hardly the actual birth of a child! Mary was facing disgrace.

What did she do? The gospel writers do not say. What is known is that an angel appeared to Joseph in his sleep and straightened all that out. Was Mary possibly praying hard that her beloved husband-to-be would be enlightened? She humbly put everything in the hands of God, knowing that shame must not come upon her child. She did not offer her own solution for her predicament. She left it up to the Almighty, who instructed Joseph to take his betrothed into his home, which he did.

After about six months, as she neared the time for her delivery, the Roman world is thrown into a great upheaval by the emperor who ordered that a census be taken by having everyone return to their hometown. In the case of Joseph, that meant Bethlehem, for he was of the house of David (Luke 2:1–5).

This meant that Mary, already in the uncomfortable position of a nine-month-pregnant mother, was going to have to undertake an arduous journey from Nazareth to Bethlehem in the middle of winter. Travel was not by a heated coach in those days. As often seen in paintings of the Nativity, Mary was most likely bundled up on a donkey with Joseph plodding alongside, hoping the dumb animal would not slip or otherwise cause injury to mother or Child. It must have taken a strong act of courage for Mary to comply with the command of a willful civil ruler and head for places unknown when her own time for needing help was drawing near. But she put consideration for her husband ahead of her own comfort and meekly went with him on this difficult journey to Bethlehem.

"While they were there, the time came for her to have her child . . . " (Lk. 2:6). Tradition and two millennia of artists, poets, and the imaginations of the faithful have depicted the concern of both Mary and Joseph that this birth take place without mishap. Worrying about her time to deliver, searching helplessly for proper shelter, being rebuffed at every turn until finding slight solace in a cave set aside for animals, Mary humbly followed the guidance of Joseph. **. . . and she gave birth to her firstborn son. She wrapped him in swaddling clothes and laid him in a manger, because there was no room for them in the inn.** (Lk. 2:7).

We can be sure that Mary prepared diligently for the birth of her Son. Having been refused succor in the town's inn and finding herself sharing quarters with smelly beasts, she took extra care in wrapping her newborn babe in clean clothes and laying Him in a food trough for the animals.

Does she have a premonition that one day this same body and blood will be offered on another wooden instrument for the salvation of souls? Does she foresee that this body and blood will be offered as food on other mangers and altars?

Such lofty thoughts might have occupied her mind. But for sure, she once again manifested her humility by accepting the lot the Lord had given her and made the most of it with tenderness and resignation.

When the angels went away from them to heaven, the shepherds said to one another, "Let us go, then, to Bethlehem to see this thing that has taken place, which the Lord has made known to us." So they went in haste and found Mary and Joseph, and the infant lying in the manger. (Lk. 2:15–16).

We can imagine the consternation in the heart of Mary at the arrival of these poor shepherds, accompanied, no doubt, by a few of their charges—the sheep they tended. Since this was the refuge for animals, she must have humbly moved over and made room for them. Her senses must have taken in the earthy sight and smell of these intruders, but she would not recoil at that, for she was really the one not to be expected there.

But then ... **they made known the message that had been told them about this child ... And Mary kept all these things, reflecting on them in her heart.** (Lk. 2:17–19). Mary could at once understand why the poor shepherds had hastened to see this wondrous event. She had herself hastened to verify the extraordinary news about her cousin Elizabeth. She could sympathize with their perhaps brusque request to gaze upon her infant Son. Humbly and lovingly, then, Mary shared the joy of her firstborn Son with these simple townsfolk who had been filled themselves with joy at the singing of the angels.

It did not bother Mary that she was surrounded at this momentous moment with dirty animals and unkempt animal watchers. She did not long for the finery and festivities that accompanied the deliveries of her relatives and friends. She accepted that this is what the Lord wanted of her, so she wanted nothing else.

But her sharing was not yet over. **"When Jesus was born in Bethlehem of Judea, in the days of King Herod, behold, magi from the east arrived in Jerusalem ... And behold, the star that they had seen at its rising preceded them, until it came and stopped over the place where the child was ... and on entering the house they saw the child with Mary his mother"** (Matthew 2:1, 9, 11).

More unexpected guests arrived in this humble first abode of the Lord Jesus. First, the poorest of laborers in the form of shepherds and their sheep. Now, the finest of wise men with their glittering entourage. Apparently, all are sent to pay homage to the Messiah, regardless of class distinction.

Mary welcomed them into her sparse surroundings, as **They prostrated themselves and did him homage. Then they opened their treasures and offered him gifts of gold, frankincense, and myrrh.** (Mt. 2:11). Mary did not, in false humility, declare that these gifts were just too much for herself or her Son. She submitted her will to all things that the Lord ordained.

A Brief Conversation with Mary

Sweet mother Mary, thank you for this lesson on humility. What an inspiration you are to me in times of trouble. You calmly left things up to the Lord, instead of dashing about helter-skelter, trying every which way to unravel problems, as I typically do. Help me to acknowledge that I don't have all the answers and must learn to have more trust in the saving power of God.

This Nativity event is often summarized by the familiar phrase from St. John (Jn.3:16) **God so loved the world he gave his only son.** The reference is often worn in face painting by those who wish to show their belief in Jesus as the Messiah. I can just picture you, Mary, looking lovingly at your newborn Babe, virtually wearing the same words on your face. You wanted all the others present at this stable to focus on Jesus and not on yourself. May I be as wise in times of celebration.

Patience, humility, poverty, joy, and a myriad of virtues shine under the star of Bethlehem as you submit to the situation in which you found yourself. How often do I rebel against the situation in which I find myself? Instead of recognizing the will of God in what I face, I presume to know what would be better for me. Teach me, Mary, to put my trust in the Lord. Show me, blessed mother, the fruit of your womb, that I may see His will in the ordinary events of my life.

At Bethlehem, you taught me about an important offshoot of humility, namely, how pleasing to God is the virtue of poverty. The connection between these two virtues escaped me for a long time. But now I see, reflecting on your acceptance of the conditions surrounding you at the birth of your Son, how humility is necessary if I am to live according to the spirit of poverty. It is the big ego in me that tells me to amass worldly possessions. It is the desire to be recognized as a person of substance that motivates me to seek material comforts and luxuries. It is self-interest above all that I must first overcome if I am to shed the accouterments of a rich lifestyle.

We recall the Bethlehem story when we celebrate Christmas each year. I try not to let the glitter and hubbub of the secular season distract me from a holy Advent and Nativity joy. While accepting the tradition of giving and receiving gifts, I ask your help in doing more than I have in the past to experience the poverty aspect of your humility.

Your ease in adapting to the situation you felt in the cave or stable came from a readiness at all times to accept what the Father sends to you. Help me, I pray, not to think I am too good for any situation I face and to humbly comply with the will of God.

Reflecting on this event in your life causes me to realize that the will of God is often made known to me by the will of others. You humbly followed the lead of Joseph and even of a cruel emperor. I have to learn that God does not show me His will face-to-face. He works through others. He leads me by the hand of others. I must learn to see His will in situations controlled by others.

O Mary, keep reminding me of how small I really am. Amen.

Mary and Trips To and From Egypt

The Flight into Egypt by William Hole

We do not know whether the magi told Joseph and Mary about their discussions with Herod in Jerusalem before the star led them further on to Bethlehem. We do know that the wise men refused to play along with

Herod and returned to their homelands by a different route. Herod meanwhile had been seething with envy at the thought of a king arising in his territory, so he ordered the slaughter of male infants in the area around Bethlehem.

> **When they had departed, behold, the angel of the Lord appeared to Joseph in a dream and said, "Rise, take the child and his mother, flee to Egypt, and stay there until I tell you. Herod is going to search for the child to destroy him."** (Matthew 2:13)

We do not know how Joseph explained the sudden need to leave Bethlehem and its joyous Christmas celebration. All we know is that **Joseph rose and took the child and his mother by night and departed for Egypt.** (Mt. 2:14). We can imagine the many feelings that Mary must have experienced at this time. She was still full of joy at the visit of the magi and the shepherds. She was still confused as she learned how to fulfill her motherly duties in feeding and caring for the newborn Babe. She was trying to understand what Joseph told her about the urgency to leave. She was upset at having to rush out into the night while protecting an infant from the weather. She was anxious about the fear that prompted her husband to bundle them up and run for their lives, for she sensed the alarm caused by his dream.

Trusting in Joseph's guidance, Mary once again got on a burro, this time cradling her Infant as best she could, and fled to Egypt. Through all this confusion and uncertainty, she obviously put her trust in the child's stepfather and was grateful for the warning sent to them by the messenger from the Father. No arguing, no dickering, no begging for time, no questions about this foreign land of Egypt, no doubt about the seriousness of the message. Mary was again the handmaid of the Lord, putting her entire life in His hands under the guidance of Joseph, her protector. Her response was hidden, but it was full of humble obedience as they immediately followed instructions.

As in their journey to Bethlehem earlier, this flight to Egypt was through unknown territory with no comforts or assistance. Both journeys were in response to a command and, therefore, not really voluntary, except for the humble obedience which Mary always practiced. This one was even worse, though, for the threat of a vengeful Jewish ruler with murder on his mind was ever over their head. Still, Mary lovingly put her life in the hands of the will of God, guided by her husband, with the confidence that comes from knowingly adhering to God's will.

Mary had been a stranger in Bethlehem, and now she spent some time as an immigrant in the land of Egypt. Assuredly, Joseph explained to her why they had fled. She really wasn't comfortable with any of this but humbly resigned herself to doing as instructed. Still she must have worried constantly about the threat to the life of Jesus until they got the green light to return to their own homeland, for the angel had told Joseph **"flee to Egypt, and stay there until I tell you"** (Matthew 2:13).

Sure enough, **When Herod had died, behold, the angel of the Lord appeared in a dream to Joseph in Egypt and said, "Rise, take the child and his mother and go to the land of Israel, for those who sought the child's life are dead." He rose, took the child and his mother, and went to the land of Israel.** (Mt. 2:19-21).

Again, no arguing, no demurring, no delay in complying with the message of a messenger from God. The little holy family simply rose and headed for home. What abandonment of their own will to the will of the Father!

But they were not out of the woods yet. For . . . **when he heard that Archelaus was ruling over Judea in place of his father Herod, he was afraid to go back there. And because he had been warned in a dream, he departed for the region of Galilee. He went and dwelt in a town called Nazareth . . .** (Mt. 2:22-23).

Poor Mary. All she wanted to do was to nurse her Infant Son and begin a simple married life with her devoted husband. We can imagine the temptation to blame all this upheaval on Joseph and his dreams, but Mary was intent on following the instructions from on high, knowing that her offspring was of the Lord and would therefore be protected by Him. As always, she submitted to these instructions.

ARTHUR X. DEEGAN II, PHD

A Brief Conversation with Mary

Sweet mother Mary, thank you for this lesson on humility. How often do I hesitate to follow what I know to be the will of God? How often do I feel the need to stop and question and turn things over in my mind over and over before finally acknowledging the wisdom of some advice or revelation given to me about my behavior?

Help me not to be foolhardy but also not to act as though I have got to have 100% certainty about the wisdom of some recommended course of action. I know how to discern God's will for me, so help me to do exactly that and not to challenge every inspiration that comes to me from our loving Father.

Who has not faced upheavals in their life? I have had major course corrections in mine. With the help of an understanding family, mirroring the trust you had in St. Joseph's ability to see you through difficult times, I really have had it easy in making life adjustments. For this, I am grateful to the Lord and to you for I know you have taken special care to oversee my life decisions.

I cannot, from personal experience, appreciate your discomfort and unease as a foreigner in new lands. I hear enough these days about the plight of countless displaced persons forced to seek asylum in foreign lands to begin to understand a little of their needs. As immigrants, they face all sorts of contradictory feelings on the part of their new neighbors, from loving hospitality on one hand to outright fear and hatred on the other. Help me to appreciate the hurt and dire straits suffered by many well-meaning refugees, dreading to be treated as if they were the barbaric terrorists who have infiltrated their number, through no fault of their own. They must have a special place in your heart, and so they must in mine.

In all these wearisome trips, you placed yourself in the loving care of your husband, St. Joseph. He is the man on the outskirts, standing in the shadows, silently waiting here when wanted and always ready to help. What an additional model for me in living the hidden life. For me, as a husband and a father, he is always my best model of behavior, which in his case was always to be the man who sets aside all thought of self and shoulders his responsibilities bravely—and obeys.

What a wise man Joseph was. He knew his place. He was the head of your little family according to the culture of the Jewish people. Yet he understood by now that his spouse was so much more beloved of God and that his Child was the Son of the Most High. Adroitly, he managed to maintain his position of leadership while accepting his real role of guardian of his two treasures, you and Jesus. Thank you, Mary, for putting yourself in the hands of Joseph and helping him fulfill his role.

O Mary, keep reminding me of how small I really am. Amen.

The Naming and the Presentation of the Infant

When eight days were completed for his circumcision, he was named Jesus, the name given him by the angel before he was conceived in the womb. (Luke 2:21)

Unlike the controversy arising at the naming of John the Baptist (Luke 1:57–66), the naming of Jesus was a very placid event, as recorded in this one sentence in the gospel of Luke. The evangelist is careful to say that the name given was not a choice of the Infant's mother but once more was at the behest of the messenger of the Lord. Mary was thus deprived of one of the joys of parenting. This event was carried out in fulfillment of the Law of Moses. Mary's total reliance on obeying the will of God is once again very clear.

We turn now to another requirement of the law, the Presentation. **When the days were completed for their purification according to the law of Moses, they took him up to Jerusalem to present him to the Lord.** (Lk. 2:22)

Nothing had been said about this by the angel at the Annunciation nor by any of the angels appearing to Joseph in his dreams. But Mary and Joseph knew well the dictates of their Jewish faith. On the other hand, Mary might well have wondered, "Purification? This Infant is the very Son of God. He was conceived by the overshadowing of the Holy Spirit. He is purity itself. How can anyone purify Him? As for me: am I not blessed among all women? I have given birth to the Son of God. What further blessing do I need?"

She *might* have thought that. But she probably did not. That would be thinking only of herself. That would be an act of pride. Mary simply obeyed the law of her ancestors. Obedience to this law flows from her humility.

She might also have thought, *The circumcision of my child is a sign of obedience to the law. But my Son is the creator of the law. He can hardly be expected to show obedience to it!* She *might* have thought that. But she probably did not, for her Son would yield to far worse than that as the Messiah.

There were three distinct things taking place at this visit to the temple. First, the mother of a male child was considered impure for a total of thirty days, precluding her from participating in worship. To totally purify her blood, she must present a purification sacrifice. In the case of the poor, two young pigeons or turtle doves would suffice. Again, Mary *could* have thought she was surely an exception to this rule, but her humility would not permit that. So she presented herself. And because her family was definitely among the poor, she presented two small birds. All this is a stellar example of Mary's humbling herself before the Lord.

The second event was to comply with the law **Every male that opens the womb shall be consecrated to the Lord.** (Lk. 2:23 and Ex. 13:2. 12) The idea here is that such a child belongs to God and must be redeemed by his parents. Five shekels was the customary price of redemption. Luke says nothing about the parents of Jesus making such a redeeming gesture. Instead, we see a third transaction taking place. Jesus is offered to the Lord as a complete commitment.

The law did not require an appearance in the temple for these acts of purification. But Mary and

Joseph chose to go to the temple, not to buy back their Son but to dedicate Him entirely to the Lord in His holy temple. This committing of the firstborn was the third element in this presentation. Thus, they *presented* Jesus, the word meaning an offering as in a sacrifice. Mary, the new mother, must have been deeply contorted at having to make this offering of her Son. Here she was to nurture and protect the Son of God Himself, and here she was giving Him up totally in the temple. Her humble submission to what was expected of her according to the law won out over her personal human feelings.

The greater part of the telling of the story of this presentation revolves around two other servants of the Lord at the temple, each of whom has a special message for Mary. The first of these was a righteous and devout man named Simeon. He must have been very pleasing to God because he had been assured of seeing the Messiah of the Lord before his death (Luke 2:25–26).

Taking the Child in his hands and giving thanks to the Lord for this spectacular sight, he then addressed the Child's mother: **"Behold, this child is destined for the fall and rise of many in Israel, and to be a sign that will be contradicted (and you yourself a sword shall pierce) so that the hearts of many may be revealed"** (Luke 2:34–35).

Mary may have understood the first part of this statement as having something to do with the mission spoken of by Gabriel. But the next phrase, recorded by Luke in parentheses as some kind of incidental consequence, hurt her to the quick. She began to feel a sword twisting in her heart. She conjured up memories of her arduous journey to Bethlehem, of the fearful escape from a vengeful Herod, of days lived as an immigrant among foreigners. She wondered if there can be anything worse yet to befall her humble family. Frightening as these thoughts might be, she said nothing, but this off-the-cuff remark about a sword will haunt Mary for thirty-three years.

The second temple habitué was the prophetess Anna who never left the temple. **And coming forward at that time, she gave thanks to God and spoke about the child to all who were awaiting the redemption of Jerusalem.** (Lk. 2:38) Now here was a redemption that Mary could identify with. These words of Anna recalled those of Gabriel saying her child will be great and He will rule over the house of Jacob forever.

At this point, the purpose of the visit to the temple has been completed, and the holy family went home. What mixed emotions filled the heart of Mary? On the one hand, she was going to feel a sword piercing her heart because of the reaction of the people to her Son; on the other hand, her Son was going to become the ruler of the throne of David. What would the future be like with this Son? Mary simply put her trust in the Lord God and left it all up to Him.

THE HIDDEN LIFE OF MARY

A Brief Conversation with Mary

Sweet mother Mary, thank you for this lesson on humility. How often do I balk at obeying what is clearly something expected of me? Maybe I don't outright disobey, but I surely find myself making excuses for myself when a little effort would be all I need to comply. You have shown me that obedience is the active part of your humility. Obeying God was not an abstract idea for you; on the contrary, it was the daily fabric of your existence. Of course you would present Jesus to the priests; that was the law of God. Help me to see that I can be humbly obedient in more ways than obeying codified laws. I obey God each time I welcome a good inspiration, each time I say no to the pleasures of the flesh, each time I see Jesus in the face of a panhandler. There is almost no moment, no action, in my daily life that cannot be transformed into an act of loving obedience to the Father.

    I have tried to reason why spiritual writers say that one act of obedience is more meritorious than all other virtuous acts put together. I think you are showing me that he who does not obey is not motivated from holiness but from pride, for it goes without saying that he who does not obey thinks himself better than others, or above the law, so to speak.

    I pray daily that I surrender my will to that of the Father. I thank Him for the knowledge and the gift of the divine will. I see you, Mary, time and time again doing this, surrendering your own will to that of the Father. All I have to do, with a little recollection and concentration, is to ask that inspiring question: What would Jesus do? What would Mary in her humility do? If I love you and Jesus, I will act as He did, so that He could say: **"I always do what is pleasing to him"** (John 8:29), and **"My food is to do the will of the one who sent me"** (John 4:34). Only then will I be able to hear the words spoken to Jesus at His baptism: **"You are my beloved Son; with you I am well pleased"** (Mark 1:11).

Help me also to realize that if I am to follow Jesus, I need to commit myself totally to Him and to recommit myself continually. I guess that is what the concept of perpetual renewal means.

You could hardly believe you heard correctly when the righteous Simeon, who was looking for the consolation of Israel (Luke 2:25), spoke aloud that his prayer had been answered. You were taken aback by the words of Anna, who was hoping for the redemption of Jerusalem and told you that day had come. Your humility would not permit you to think you were the center of these holy words.

As I contemplate this presentation in the temple, I feel that the most lasting remembrance you had of it were the words of Simeon about a sword piercing your heart. It seems totally unfair that he was not more open in this prediction. What sword? Where? When? How? But yours was to quietly and humbly accept the words of a holy man and ponder them.

We are told that Simeon was a righteous man. Righteousness in the language of the Old Testament was the term for fidelity to the Torah, to the Word of God. It meant observance of the right path, shown by God, with the Ten Commandments at its center. The term in the New Testament corresponding to the Old Testament concept of righteousness is *faith*. You were more righteous than Simeon or any other holy person, so you accepted this warning because of your trust in God.

This was just the first time you had to ponder words whose meaning would become clear only years later. We have been told that the Greek word for ponder, *sumballousa*, literally means "piecing together." As if you didn't have enough to do as a new teenage mother. It would take quite an effort to piece all this together. But you were content with that challenge being given to you. You recalled Gabriel advising, "Do not be afraid." Placing yourself in the hands of God, you dutifully awaited further expectations of you.

You were just starting out here, but you made it a point to begin in the temple of the Lord. May I continue to find courage in my local house of the Lord. While I am no longer just starting out, I can still try to imitate your courage in facing the future, whatever it might hold for me.

O Mary, keep reminding me of how small I really am. Amen.

The Holy Family in Nazareth

When they had fulfilled all of the prescriptions of the law of the Lord, they returned to Galilee, to their own town of Nazareth. The child grew and became strong, filled with wisdom; and the favor of God was upon him. (Luke 2:39–40)

In Luke's account, these two verses summarize the life of Jesus, Mary, and Joseph from the presentation in the temple until the pilgrimage to Jerusalem when the child was twelve years old. The details of their life there remain hidden indeed.

St. Matthew's gospel sheds a little light on how they happened to choose Nazareth. Joseph received another visit from an angel to tell him that Herod had died and so it was safe to return to Israel from the obscurity of Egypt. Another backbreaking trek across unfamiliar land, plodding day and night with no provisions or comfort of any sort, all in humble obedience to a message from the Lord. But when Joseph learned that Herod's son, Archelaus, reputed to be more wicked than his father, was king, he did not stay in Judea but chose Nazareth in Galilee as their residence (Matthew 2:19–23).

This was to be the home of the Holy Family for almost thirty years. We know that Joseph provided for his family by being a carpenter (Matthew 13:55). But other than that, we can only assume how Mary spent her days as a dutiful bride and mother and how Jesus spent His days being brought up in the care of His Jewish parents.

Many authors theorize, for lack of any written account, that Mary spent her time as a dutiful wife and mother. Her fine and skillful hands worked only for Joseph and Jesus. The fine garments she made, the tasty meals she prepared were for them; the home she kept so clean out of love for them. With her kind voice, she spoke to them; with her loving eyes, she looked upon them. In a word, with what reverence, devotion, perfection, and piety must not Mary have served them during those years (cf. "The Mother of Christ" by Fr. Clerment Beck, SVD, writing for Catholics online for the Third Millennium). Some have gone so far as to sum up the life of Mary as "Occupation: Homemaker."

Pope Saint John Paul II spoke of what took place in this hidden life: "Mary's awareness that she was carrying out a task entrusted to her by God gave a higher meaning to her daily life. The simple, humble chores of everyday life took on special value in her eyes, since she performed them as a service to Christ's mission" (Pope John Paul II, catechesis, February 5, 1997, page 11, as reported in L'Osservatore Romano, the newspaper of the Holy See). Clearly the hidden life meant a life of humble service.

Pope Paul VI spoke on the feast of the holy family about the home of Nazareth as the school where we begin to understand the life of Jesus, the school of the gospel. First a lesson of silence, a lesson on family life and the communion of love, a lesson of work, a lesson of self-sacrifice (cf. Pope Paul VI at Nazareth, January 5, 1964). How well Mary learned those lessons.

Pope Benedict XVI prayed, "At the decisive hour in your own life, you said, 'Here I am, the servant of the Lord' (Luke 1:38). You lived your whole life as service. And you continue to do so throughout history" (Pope Benedict XVI, prayer before the Marian column in Munich, September 7, 2006).

True humility becomes such a habit that it marks one's entire life as it did for Mary.

As for her interior life, **He went down with them and came to Nazareth, and was obedient to them; and his mother kept all these things in her heart** (Luke 2:51–52). Mary kept these things in two ways: she reflected and prayed on them, and she lived them in her daily life—a life centered on Jesus and the fulfillment of her part in our salvation history by preparing Jesus for His public life. How could she do that? By being what all mothers are: a source of health and strength, a source of wisdom and learning, a close comforter and adviser, a loving companion.

If Mary had to, on occasion, correct the behavior of her adolescent Son, which was something she must do in training Him to avoid the perils of life, this must have tested her humility. This was her Lord she was raising, and she was always the servant of the Lord. But her calling as mother was to say what had to be said to an errant child. That would take even more humility.

Another virtue, that of prudence, cultivated and sustained by her memory of Simeon's words, embraced the whole span of her earthly life but was practiced especially during the years of silence and hiddenness spent in Nazareth. It is related to humility because it is based on the admission that one does not know everything. Much less, in this case, did Mary know when the sword of Simeon would pierce her heart. She had fled from the ravages of Herod over the Holy Innocents; she had spent time as an immigrant in Egypt, wondering what was awaiting them around the next bend. When would the peace and tranquility of life in Nazareth come to a horrible end? Mary had to be prudent in protecting her divine Son from any evil that might be lurking in the shadows.

Hear Pope Saint John Paul II again: "In relating these brief remarks about Jesus' life, Luke is probably referring to Mary's memories of a period of profound intimacy with her Son. The union between Jesus and the one who was 'full of grace' goes far beyond what normally exists between mother and child, because it is rooted in a particular supernatural condition and reinforced by the special conformity of both to the divine will." The hidden life is therefore a life of deepest humility.

Every day of intimacy with Him is an invitation to know Him better, to discover more deeply the meaning of His presence and the mystery of His person. Mary was busy with all the things that went with being a mother and a spouse. But her attention on Jesus was such that she saw and heard nothing but Jesus as the center of her life. She was totally absorbed with Him. She was the mother, but watching over her Son, she learned from Him every day.

Thus we can conclude that the atmosphere of tranquility and peace in the house of Nazareth and their constant seeking to fulfill God's plan was in great measure due to the humility of Mary.

THE HIDDEN LIFE OF MARY

A Brief Conversation with Mary

Sweet mother Mary, thank you for this lesson on humility. Your example enlightens and encourages the experience of so many women who carry out their daily tasks exclusively in the home. It is a question of a humble, hidden, repetitive effort and is often not sufficiently appreciated. Nonetheless, the long years you spent in the house of Nazareth reveal the enormous potential of genuine love and, thus, of salvation. In fact, the simplicity of the lives of so many housewives, seen as a mission of service and love, is of extraordinary value in the Lord's eyes. Help me to appreciate that in the lives of all the women I have been blessed to know and love.

For all those years of the hidden life in Nazareth, you were occupied with learning how to surrender to the will of the Father and His only Son, Jesus. You were in His presence and absorbed His message of love and forgiveness. I do not have Him physically beside me all day long, but I still wish to be in the presence of God always, and I can with your help. For the true presence of God is, to speak exactly, nothing but a sort of forgetfulness of creatures with a secret desire of finding God. It is in this that interior and exterior divine silence consists, so precious, so desirable, and so profitable: the true earthly paradise, where as a soul that loves God, I can enjoy already a foretaste of heavenly joy.

I cannot live my external life the same way you did, for our times are so different from yours. But I can reflect on how so many others exhibited that same simplicity of spirit in their different circumstances. I think of the poor widow, giving only a farthing, yet giving more than all the rest; and the publican, turning from sin to God and with a full heart, crying, **"O God, be merciful to me a sinner"** (Luke 18:13); and the prodigal coming back to his father, with his **"Father, I have sinned against heaven and against you. I no longer deserve to be called your son"** (Luke 15:18–19); and the woman who washed the Lord's feet with her tears and to whom many sins were forgiven because she loved much (Luke 7:37–38); and the little children who turned to Him with pure hearts and trustful eyes, and whom He set before us as our model, for of such is the kingdom of heaven (Matthew 18:3). All these practiced humility after your example. So can I, with your help.

My life is and will be very insignificant in the world order of things. This ought not to discourage me. There is no need for notoriety outside my small group of family and friends. Help me, Mary, to imitate you as you lived the sentiment in the Psalm: **Teach me to do your will, for you are my God** (Psalm 143:10).

What is most amazing about your humility is the way you took everything in stride. You endured toil and grief and dangers and poverty and want and terror and the rage of the wicked king and the unending flights, all by a humble submission to the will of

God. And you smiled through it all: full of joy in what you did, prompt in obedience, devoted in your service, with nary a concern for your own comfort, as though you were not doing anything special at all.

If you had not shown me how to do this, I would never have conceived that just living my ordinary life with its small demands would be anything meritorious.

O Mary, keep reminding me of how small I really am. Amen.

The Pilgrimage to Jerusalem

As faithful adherents to the Law of Moses, **Each year his parents went to Jerusalem for the feast of Passover, and when he was twelve years old, they went up according to festival custom** (Luke 2:41).

This particular pilgrimage was mentioned by Luke because on the way home, after a day, Mary realized that Jesus was not with her or any of their relatives. We say, "Jesus was lost." What agony for His mother. How could she not know where He was? How could she have allowed the Pearl of great price to get lost? What kind of a mother was she? Instead of being blessed, would she now be cursed? Such thoughts of self-chastisement *might* have plagued the now twenty-something-year-old maiden. But rather than wallowing in self-pity, Mary's humility had her face the facts and then carefully address them in an organized manner.

Working their way back to Jerusalem, Mary and Joseph went to the last place they could remember being with the Boy and **found him in the temple, sitting in the midst of the teachers, listening to them and asking them questions, and all who heard him were astounded at his understanding and his answers** (Luke 2:46). *Thank God*, thinks Mary. *All is not lost. Here he is. But what is He doing?* Mary and Joseph **"were astonished"** at the scene before them. Even though they knew He was the Son of God, they could hardly expect Him to be astounding the learned teachers in the temple of the Lord. Mary was humble herself and expected her Son to act in like manner. Which did not include lecturing to the priests!

But an even stronger feeling took charge, and like any dutiful mother, Mary addressed Jesus, **"Son, why have you done this to us? Your father and**

I have been looking for you with great anxiety" (Luke 2:48). She is scolding Him. Yet she knows better than to make an issue of how He was behaving with these teachers—that would not be for her to judge. The reason for her anxiety was truly that Jesus had caused both of His parents to be concerned over His safety. That was more in keeping with her acceptance of her duties toward Him. Then, too, like a wise parent, Mary's first words were an opportunity for Jesus to explain what He had done by remaining behind. **"Why have you done this?"** Might there be a reason for this? Humility mandated that she not jump to conclusions about this strange behavior. Jesus may be kind of lost from her physical presence, but Jesus never left the heart of Mary.

Given the opportunity to explain, Jesus answers, **"Why were you looking for me? Did you not know that I must be in my Father's house?"** (Luke 2:49). Not a very convincing justification for the three-day absence from the care of His parents. And in a way, this answer was like pointing the finger at someone else as being responsible. His parents should have known better! Most parents would hardly let a child get away with that. But Mary, always submitting to the will of God—even as expressed by angels and a husband, and now a Son, in ways she could not readily comprehend—accepts this explanation and says no more. **They did not understand what he said to them** (Luke 2:50). The point had been made by Jesus, and it would be up to her to figure it out. Mary had long since accepted her unworthiness to be the mother of Jesus and did not wonder that she did not fully know what the mission of Jesus was. She did not feel that the chastiser had become the chastised; that would be feeling sorry for herself and just not Mary's style.

Jesus also knew He had made His point, for **He went down with them and came to Nazareth, and was obedient to them . . . And Jesus advanced [in] wisdom and age and favor before God and man** (Luke 2:51–52).

As Jesus grew in wisdom, age, and grace, Mary understood better the meaning of her own motherhood and her hidden life. **. . . and his mother kept all these things in her heart.** (Lk. 2:51). Many writers have said Mary kept these things in two ways: first, she pondered over them, to *ponder* meaning even to argue with oneself as to the true meaning of it all; and second, she kept them by her actions of compliance. Once again, humility called for her to accept the will of God while trying to wrap her simple human mind around it all.

In the dignified and hardworking atmosphere of Nazareth, Mary strove to understand the workings of Providence in her Son's mission. A subject of particular reflection for His mother, in this regard, was certainly the statement Jesus had made in the temple.

Mary recalled often how erudite her Son had appeared with the wise teachers. And while she must have been proud of her Son and how He was received by them, her response was a response, not of pride, but of love and commitment which was made discretely and kept in a little village in the middle of nowhere for another eighteen or so years.

A Brief Conversation with Mary

Sweet mother Mary, thank you for this lesson on humility. Help me to imitate the simplicity of life you lived in the hidden life at Nazareth. Looking at Nazareth, contemplating the mystery of the hidden life of Jesus and yourself, I see how you are the perfect example of the mystery of our life, which St. Paul recalls **is hidden with Christ in God** (Colossians 3:3). Please teach me to follow your example of silence and prayer, which was your constant attitude all these years.

You invite me to follow your example here of meditating on the mystery of your Son. In a world filled with messages of all kinds, seeking to outdo each other in their raucous clamor for attention, you teach me to appreciate silence which fosters a rich contemplative life. When I am tempted to think that my life is worthless because it is insignificant, you have revealed how valuable a simple life can be if lived for love of you and your divine Son.

I am besieged on every side by many voices, loud and subtle, drowning out the idealism of your hidden life. Help me to resist the familiar, popular values and viewpoints which would undermine my effort to follow your example. I do not have to live in a small town like Nazareth to live your life of simplicity and focus on the will of God.

Then there is the loudest voice of all, blaring so loud in my desire to contemplate in silence. I think it was Pope Benedict who called it the malady of the "I." I know that distraction well. I so often put the creature in place of the Creator. I bow down to the work of my hands (Isaiah 2:8), letting thoughts of the work of my hands interrupt my contemplation of you and your Son. Be it the children I am proud of, the lectures I give, the book I write, the investments I make. All these destroy the solitude required for living a hidden life. All these are manifestations of the big "I." There it is again: my self taking first place in the center of my world. Will I ever learn to be humble?

O Mary, keep reminding me of how small I really am. Amen.

Mary and the Wedding at Cana

The simple and gratifying life of Nazareth prepared both mother and Son for what must eventually take place: the public mission of the Word made flesh. Mary may have gradually worried less and less about the sword that would one day pierce her heart. She had long since entirely left that in the hands of God and continued to live her life as one of assisting in the preparation of Jesus for His ministry.

As the years went by, the Holy Family lived a peaceful life, keeping faith with the Father by observing all the laws, working by the sweat of their brow to provide a humble lifestyle, and enjoying the limited social life available in a small town. And so it was that one day **there was a wedding in Cana in Galilee, and the mother of Jesus was there. Jesus and his disciples were also invited to the wedding** (John 2:1–2).

The reference to disciples is a way of putting this event in the context of the gradual shift in the way Jesus began to spend His time. The strong thirty-year-old Son in the family had begun to acquire new friends who looked up to Him and followed Him as a teacher. He had even been baptized publicly by John the Baptist, attracting the attention of onlookers. But here we are interested in what happens between Jesus and His mother at this wedding.

When the wine ran short, the mother of Jesus said to him, 'They have no wine' (John 2:3). Putting aside any discussion of the length and type celebration this must have been, we see Mary become aware of what could be a big embarrassment to her host. We do not know whether Mary was a close relative, a close friend, or even part of a group responsible for the catering as a reason for her apparent alarm at this predicament.

Putting that aside also, we know that those who are humble are quick to recognize those who are in need because they are not thinking of themselves all the time. Here we see Mary's maternal affectionate concern for others, namely, the bridal couple hosts. She became aware of their problem and immediately wished to rectify the situation. She did not do so in any busybody way that irritates people in such a gathering. Rather she simply turned to her Son with a matter-of-fact statement.

Mary left everything to the judgment of Jesus, just as she left everything up to what Gabriel said was the will of God. She did not ask for any particular action on the part of Jesus. She was aware of His beginning to appear in public and did not hesitate to put Him in a position to be seen by others, if that was OK with Him. This had become her permanent way of seeing things. She taught us here how to pray. We learn readiness to help and the humility of leaving it all up to God.

What she probably did not expect was a somewhat curt reply. **Jesus said to her, 'Woman, how does your concern affect me? My hour has not yet come'** (John 2:4). One would expect a loving son to address her as "mother," not as "woman." As with everything Jesus did, the word had depth of meaning. The term "woman" looked both backward and forward, just as it would do when Jesus used the same word in addressing His mother from the cross on Calvary. It was a reminder that Mary was to be recognized as the new Eve, symbol of all women, cooperating in the restoration of all humanity into a state of grace. And it prepared her to be the refuge of all future children of God when He made her the mother of us all. Mary was the mother of Jesus, yes, but she was also to be the progenitor of all the children of God, especially in His church.

Though Jesus seemed to be saying no to her implied request, Mary knew she would forever be the intermediary of all petitions to her Son. And as a petitioner herself, then, her only next thought was to subordinate her view of what must be done to the will of her divine Son and rely on Him to do what He thought best. So **His mother said to the servers, 'Do whatever he tells you'** (John 2:5). As far as we know, Mary then turned her attention to other things. We hear nothing further about her part in the miracle Jesus then performed **"as the beginning of his signs in Cana in Galilee and so revealed his glory"** (John 2:11).

We do hear that the chief steward and the host exult at their good fortune at having a superlative kind of wine for the balance of their celebration. And who was responsible for that? Jesus, of course. But who put Him up to it, even at first against His better judgment, so to speak? His mother. And was she to get any thanks for this? None that we know of, unlike the typical person's care to let everyone know how instrumental they are in solving any problem, Mary's humility kept her in the shadows. God's plan was that Mary be involved in all aspects of our salvation. No wonder then that she was part of the first manifestation of the glory of Jesus.

A Brief Conversation with Mary

Sweet mother Mary, thank you for this lesson in humility. I know how I bristle if I am not recognized for any little good thing that I do. I see now that if I follow you, I must be content to remain in the shadows.

There is no indication in the gospel story that you made known that you were responsible for this good deed. Being successful at something is hard to remain silent about. Help me to practice a couple of what have been recorded as ten resolutions of Pope Saint John XXIII (Magnificat, October, 2007, P 154–155):

- I will do one good deed and not tell anyone about it.
- I will do at least one thing I do not like doing, and if my feelings are hurt, I will make sure that no one notices.

Teach me to pray to Jesus as you did in Cana. Encourage me to keep asking for my needs and those of others, even if at first the Lord does not seem inclined to listen. I know the door will be opened if I keep knocking. I also know, from your example here, that you know what I need even before I ask and that you are at my side, ready to intervene. But you still want me to humble myself and assume the position of begging. May I humbly assume the "orandi" stance of outstretched hands, a position of praying going all the way back to carvings in the catacombs.

I hear you, Mary, telling me, "Do whatever he tells you." And I accept this good advice. He tells me things in sacred scripture, He speaks through the ministers at the altar, He joins the Holy Spirit in whispering to my soul, He speaks through my guardian angel's guidance, and He is eloquent in the looks of those I encounter in the world every day. Open my eyes and ears to hear Jesus speak to me.

And please confirm me in the realization that I need you to plead for my needs and intentions as you did for the host at Cana. Yes, I always need you when I am approaching Jesus. I need you to turn to Him, speak to Him, pray to Him, and advocate for me. In a word, I need you so that I may always do God's holy will and seek His greater glory in everything I do.

O Mary, keep reminding me of how small I really am. Amen.

Mary during the Public Life of Jesus

After the wedding at Cana, the gospels seem to close the book on Mary. We have heard her speak seven times, the sum total of all her words in scripture. Her humility has shone forth as her words let us see into her immaculate heart.

- **"How can this be, since I have no relations with a man?"** (Luke 1:34)
- **"Behold, I am the handmaid of the Lord. May it be done to me according to your word"** (Luke 1:38)
- the greeting to Elizabeth;
- the Magnificat (Luke 1:46–55)
- **"Son, why have you done this to us? Your father and I have been looking for you with great anxiety"** (Luke 2:48)
- **"They have no wine"** (John 2:3)
- **"Do whatever he tells you"** (John 2:5)

Jesus clearly left home and began extensive travels. That meant He left His mother. What mother finds it easy to see her son leave the nest? Mary was so close to her Son that this must have been an early sword piercing her heart. But she knew for years that the day was coming, so she humbly accepted the separation as the will of God. In her heart, she already accepted the later teaching of Jesus that anyone who clung to family before Him was not worthy of Him.

No one knows how much time Mary spent following Jesus in His public ministry. Pope Saint John Paul II says that Mary sometimes heard her Son's preaching (cf. General Audience of Wednesday, March 12, 1997). Her desire to be close to Him must have been very strong. It must have compelled her to leave home and follow His constant travel. If the Son of Man had nowhere to lay His head, that would be good enough for Mary. We know she was along with Him part of the time. For example, three gospels report an instance when Mary and the relatives of Jesus send word to Him that they would like to speak to Him (Matthew 12:46–50, Mark 3:31–35, Luke 8:19–21).

The context would seem to indicate that Jesus had already been experiencing threats and opposition to His teaching despite the many cures and good works He was already providing to those of open minds. We can infer that Mary and the others were getting anxious for the safety of Jesus. People were already thinking of doing Him harm. Perhaps Mary had been present at that other synagogue when His enemies rose up and put Him out of the city and led Him to the brow of the hill in order to murder Him (Luke 4:29–30). Perhaps, in keeping with His instructions to His disciples, He had occasion to leave an area by shaking the dust off His feet as a sign of displeasure with their lack of receptivity, causing Mary once again to fear for His life.

At any rate, here they were, outside a place thought to perhaps be a home where He was staying, where Jesus was speaking to a crowd. Because of the numbers, they could not get close to Him, so they sent a message, a request to speak to Him. Had this happened before? Had they been following Him as He proceeded from town to town, curing the sick and preaching repentance? Did He know what they wanted to tell Him? All we know for sure is that Jesus took advantage of this opportunity to explain to His listeners that His mother and brother and sister were those who do the will of God. All three evangelists use the very same words in quoting this reply of Jesus. It must have struck a very deep chord in their mind. Jesus was making a very important point, and all three gospels reported it clearly.

The question for us is: Was this a rebuke by Jesus? There is no indication that He did meet with His mother at this request. Rebuke may be too strong a word for it, but no one reported that He did meet with Mary at this time. Perhaps He was saying, "Once before I told you my time had not yet come. Well, now it has come, and I am carrying out the mission for which I was sent to earth through you."

What was Mary's reaction? She apparently did not insist. She most assuredly would have agreed with the words Jesus used to His listeners. She was learning that He had come to establish a new relationship between the people and their Lord. She was learning that she must share Him with so many others, even those who were slow to believe. Since she was following Him as an itinerant preacher, she was becoming convinced that her role as sole possessor of the Messiah was over. That was a big test for her humility. The treasure was not hers alone any more. That took courage and love and humility to accept. And Mary did!

On another occasion, **while he was speaking, a woman from the crowd called out and said to him, 'Blessed is the womb that carried you and the breasts at which you nursed.' He replied, 'Rather,**

blessed are those who hear the word of God and observe it' (Luke 11:27–28).

For a second time, Jesus places the bond that unites the soul with God above the natural bond of parentage which unites the mother of God with her divine Son. Jesus is not belittling the role of Mary. He is using the dignity of human motherhood, which is held in high esteem by all, as a means to make known the extra value of holiness. Jesus, therefore, really praises His mother in a most emphatic way, for she excelled the rest of men in holiness not less than in dignity.

A Brief Conversation with Mary

Sweet mother Mary, thank you for this lesson in humility. To leave the comfort of home—even a simple abode in the small town of Nazareth—to follow your Son as He labored so intensely to get people to accept His message took courage and an abandonment of your own preferences. Fueled partly by your maternal instinct to protect Him from abuse of all kinds and partly by justifiable pride in whatever recognition your Son did manage to gather, you were treated like any other of His many followers. You knew you were so much more to Him, yet you accepted humbly His need to focus elsewhere.

May I be one of the brothers He spoke about by my doing the will of God as you did so perfectly.

THE HIDDEN LIFE OF MARY

I can see you looking so intently at Him as He prayed, as He cured the sick, as He forgave sinners. You knew He was doing the work for which He became man. You saw the gratitude and returned love on the part of those He helped. As a proud mother, you basked in His glory. Yet you kept silent. Instead of proclaiming with justifiable pride that here was your Son, thus sharing in His glory, you remained silent. You quietly shared His success in the eyes of men. Just as you shared silently in His shame when others jeered Him, you remained in the shadows always.

As a loving, and justifiably proud, mother, were you ever tempted to shout to the onlookers that this was your Son? Were you tempted to try to take some of the praise He received as due to you as His mother? Nothing is ever said about your temptations. We know about the temptations received by Jesus, so you also must have been tempted. And I can just imagine the wily devil, knowing how important humility was to you, deciding to strike at that essential virtue by suggesting that you should receive some public recognition for all the good done by your Son.

But you crushed his deceitful head! You told Satan that there was no way you were going to give in to pride! You told him that Jesus, the Son of God, was hiding Himself in the form of a mere human, that the Creator of all was hidden in the form of a creature, that the Messiah allowed Himself to be cursed by His defamers. No, there was no way you were going to depart from your chosen hidden lifestyle.

As you followed Him during His public ministry, you saw the transformation that took place with so many after their personal encounter with your Son. Whether it was Mary Magdalene, the Samaritan woman, the man born blind, Zacchaeus, or the criminal on the cross next to His, Jesus caused a conversion of their heart when they met Him with an open mind and heart. Something happened. It was an event. Help me, Mary, to benefit in like manner from my encounters with Jesus. I need to be reconverted daily in my belief in my Savior.

On the other hand, you were probably very upset with the reaction of those who refused to accept Jesus and His mission. They were happy to benefit from His curative ministry as the blind became able to see and the lame became able to walk. But they did not seem to hear the message He was preaching. He told them the kingdom of God was at hand. He asked for repentance. How you must have felt like grabbing them by the nape and saying, "How ungrateful you are! Can you not see that He wants only your eternal welfare?" But you kept your thoughts to yourself. You remained in the shadows despite their ingratitude.

In my love for you and my desire for all to honor you, I am not disappointed by the little written about you during the time of the life of your Son. This was the time for Him to appear front and center and for you to remain in your chosen place of comfort, very much offstage. As one of the poets has said, "When the sun appears, even the brightest stars become invisible."

Help me, in other words, please, to grow steadily through my years in the life of holiness to which I am called by Jesus. **Be holy because I [am] holy** (1 Peter 1:16). I must never rest in this effort. I must monitor my own progress. That means concentration on the work I am doing, for that is where God is for me, without worrying about the past or the future. That is the only way to banish all tension, all anxiety, and all those useless imaginations which are so much more tiring than the work itself.

In that way, I will be lost in my effort to grow in holiness and be less self-centered.

O Mary, keep reminding me of how small I really am. Amen.

Mary and the Passion and Death of Jesus

Finally, after three years of His public ministry, and as another celebration of the Passover was drawing nigh, Jesus sent a few of His followers ahead to prepare for a meal with His closest friends (which turned out to be the last supper) in the upper room in Jerusalem. Where was Mary at this time? Certainly she would have been willing and anxious to help prepare a meal for Jesus. But there is no mention of her. From His triumphant entry into the city on a donkey amid cheering throngs of admirers strewing palm branches on His path, through the next few days when Jesus was in the city, there is no mention of Mary. When that awesome Thursday evening came and Jesus reclined at the table with His intimate disciples, there is no sign of His mother. Leonardo da Vinci shows Jesus and the twelve seated around Him. It must have been a guy thing.

When Jesus washed the feet of His Apostles, teaching them an important lesson in humility, He might have had His mother in mind as one who had an abundance of that particular virtue. When He commissioned the twelve to offer the bread of life and chalice of salvation as He did, thus instituting the Blessed Sacrament, and empowering them to bring His body and blood to others, Mary was not included. But then, she had already brought His sacred body and blood to the world through the empowerment of the Holy Spirit.

We do not know where Mary was when her beloved Son was betrayed by one of His close friends in the Garden of Gethsemane and subsequently marched from one Jewish leader to another all through that eventful night. But we can well imagine that she was not far from His side. We can picture her knowing where He was dining and then getting word of His arrest. We can be sure she tried to come to His side, probably to be brutally shoved aside by Roman soldiers and minor religious officials alike. What pain for this delicate heart! How the sword begins to pierce her heart!

Jesus was probably not the only one to go without sleep that night. As He was accused by jealous religious leaders and appointed Roman magistrates, Mary tried in vain to find Him, worrying constantly for His safety and very life. As the early hours of Friday march on, she was thrust in the midst of a crazy mob, now roiled to fever pitch by unjust Jewish officials and dastardly common folk who sought anonymity and freedom from answering for their own crimes.

And then she caught sight of Him. Or was it Him? The Roman governor appeared on a balcony and, apparently not convinced himself that Jesus was guilty, pointed to a bloodied, staggering wretch in a purple cloak with a crown of thorns digging into His scalp, and said, **"Behold, the man!"** (John 19:5). Mary could hardly contain herself and broke into tears as she caught sight of that loving face, while around her the crowd, stirred up by the priests and guards, yelled, **"Crucify him, crucify him!"** (John 19:6).

Who can fathom the depth of sorrow that plagued that loving mother's soul? Who can ever appreciate the pain caused by the sword penetrating her heart? Only Mary's unconditional yes saved her from having a stroke on the spot! Maybe she turned to those jostling her and begged them to remember all the kind things Jesus had done for them and their afflicted ones. Maybe she pleaded with a few she recognized as having been followers of her Son, hoping they could muster up some support for Jesus. Maybe she searched for Peter, the stalwart fisherman who was acknowledged by others as a leader of her Son's coterie, only to hear he had hidden himself in self-pity.

The crowd had its way, and Jesus was condemned. He was laden with the instrument of His death, a much too heavy cross which immediately forced Him to the ground. Tradition tells us (as we commemorate in the fourth station of the Way of the Cross) that Jesus made visual contact with His beleaguered mother along the way to Calvary. What did Mary see in the eyes of her Son? Gratitude for a life of service? Love that only a divine Son could have for an adoring mother? Appreciation for her loyalty? Fear that she herself might be caught up in this absurd tragedy of errors? Praise for her commitment to allow the will of the Father to carry the day contrary to her maternal instincts?

Mary found some solace in the comforting arms of a few dedicated women who helped her walk or stumble along in the wake of her Son. She almost collapsed as she saw Jesus fall time and time again under the weight of the cross. She breathed a little sigh of relief when she noticed an onlooker who seemed to have just come in from the fields somewhere being forced to carry the heavy cross ahead of Jesus. She clasped to her breast another young woman named Veronica who offered a damp towel to wipe the brow of Jesus for some momentary relief. Somehow as the terrible and terrifying band of soldiers surrounding their hapless prisoner made its way up the rugged path to the Hill of Skulls, Mary caught sight of John, the youngest follower in Jesus's little band of intimates. *Where are all the rest?* she wondered.

Just before reaching the top of the hill, Jesus stopped and spoke. He turned His attention to a group of Jewish women who were standing off to the side away from the soldiers. What will He say? Will He ask for His mother? She tried in vain to join them. But she heard His words of comfort for them and their children. How much like Him to do this? No thought about His own predicament, just constant love for others, even nonentities in His life like this anonymous little group of mothers.

Being torn away from this interlude, Jesus was roughly thrust to the top. His garments were torn from his bloodied body, causing even more excruciating pain. Mary could hardly stand it as her Son was shamefully disrobed and thrown to the ground upon the wooden bed. Her motherly heart cried out for that sacred body which she fed at her breast, clothed as an infant, and raised to manhood. What an abomination! Yet inwardly she joined Jesus as He freely accepted this unspeakable shame.

As the cruel hammer transfixed those sacred hands and feet to the cross, the sword twisted in the heart of His mother. With every blow, the sword sunk deeper. Mary's soul suffered as much interiorly as the racked body of Jesus suffered before her eyes. Then they mercilessly raised Him up by dropping the foot of the cross into a small hole, causing the mountain to shake as the tree-bearing instrument of death settled into place. What was probably a small plopping noise sounded to Mary like a thunderbolt, as she saw Jesus wince with pain.

For three hours, the body of Jesus, contorted with agonizing pain, hung against the unforgiving nails, stretching His extremities to the limit. Mary heard the last will and testament of Jesus as His voice, creaking with congestion, sounded lovingly in her ears. He begged His Father to forgive all, for they knew not what they were doing. *How can He talk about forgiveness? This is an abomination on the face of the earth!* thought Mary. But then her resignation to the will of God rejected such thoughts, and she joined her Son in forgiving not only the rabble that has caused this farce but all others down through the ages whose sins were being forgiven by the sacrifice of her Son.

She heard one of the two criminals crucified with Jesus chastise his accomplice and ask for mercy from Jesus. She understood the simple reply that faith in Him will merit an eternal reward that very day. Mary joined her Son in rejoicing that even evildoers like this man understood His message of forgiveness.

Meanwhile small cohorts of the rabble were also near the cross and taunted Jesus, mocking His claim to be the Son of God. They asked a miraculous freedom from the cross as a sign or proof that they should believe Him. Mary could only think, *What ungrateful people! How often had Jesus done exactly that: performed signs to alleviate their suffering, illness, and disease? But for Him an act of faith came first and then a sign, not the other way around. Will they never learn?* Furthermore, Mary recalled how often Jesus had told them He would not cater to their puerile demands for signs. He had said on one occasion, **"No sign will be given . . . except . . . Just as Jonah was in the belly of the whale three days and three nights, so will the Son of Man be in the heart of the earth three days and three nights"** (Matthew 12:39–40).

Then it was her turn. **When Jesus saw his mother and the disciple there whom he loved, he said to his mother, "Woman, behold, your son"**. (Jn. 19:26). There were some other women standing by the cross with Mary, but she knew to whom He was talking. As soon as she heard the word *woman*, she remembered the other time He had addressed her thus. She was being called the second Eve. She was being reminded that her role as His mother, her role in the sanctification plan of the Father, was to be the caring mother of His church, the source of strength and wisdom for all to come after Him. She understood that the young man she was arm in arm with under the cross was a stand-in for all of His followers forever. **Then he said to the disciple, "Behold, your mother"**. (Jn. 19:27). Jesus was giving His beloved mother into the hands of young John to care for.

Mary had not even given her own future well-being a single thought through all this time, in keeping with her deep humility. But had she done so, she might very well have other plans for herself. But now that Jesus had spoken, she readily accepted His will over her own and, from that hour, went with John to his own house (John 19:27).

Time and time again from the cross, Jesus was thinking of others. But now His aching human body cried out, **"My God, my God, why have you forsaken me?"** (Matthew 27:46). Another twist of the sword in Mary's heart. Jesus sounded as though He were being asked to bear more than humanly possible. And so Mary thought, *Yes, not humanly possible, but after all, this is not only my human son, but He is the Son of God. He will bear it all, and so will I, for that is the will of God.*

How long could Jesus bear the pain and disfigurement caused by His insidious position on the cross? After a while, He cried out that He thirsted. Sponge with hyssop at the tip of a spear did not seem to help much. Mary wonders if Jesus really meant to tell the world that He was thirsting for souls. Were His outstretched arms really a symbol of His welcome for all to come and join His followers? Was He indicating to what lengths He was willing to go to show His great love for all? Such were very likely His intentions, from what Mary understood of her Son and His mission. Too bad this was the price He had to pay for such followers! But then again, she thought "Jesus did not feel the price was inordinate," so she would join Him and offer the sword, now all the way through her heart, in accord with Him.

Meanwhile, the soldiers who had painfully stripped Jesus of His few garments sat nearby as though nothing important was taking place and cast lots for them (John 19:23–24). This was not lost on Mary, even though her attention was focusing on her Son. "They tear my poor Son's sacred body asunder, but they take pains not to tear his tunic! What kind of priority is this!" But her humility takes over, and she becomes resigned to part with the very vesture she had toiled in providing for Jesus as His loving mother.

At long last Jesus uttered two last phrases. He commended His spirit to the Father and exclaimed with His dying breath, **"It is finished!"** (John 19:30). Hardly had He said this than the sky blackened, thunder roared, the earth opened, and Mary learned later that the very veil of the temple was rent in two. Nature had to express its displeasure with the crucifixion of its Creator. **The centurion and the men with him who were keeping watch over Jesus feared greatly when they saw the earthquake and all that was happening, and they said "Truly, this was the Son of God."** (Mt. 27:54) Mary heard this and gave thanks that someone had recognized the folly of what had just taken place. *Too bad my Son had to give up His life before they accepted Him*, she thought. Then humbly told herself that Jesus knew the price He had to pay for a few changes of heart.

She humbly gave in to His assessment of the price and once more submitted her judgment to His.

The end had come, and the whole world quaked at the indignity of it. But there was more indignity to come. **One soldier thrust his lance into his side, and immediately blood and water flowed out** (John 19:34). Maybe Mary remembered the scripture: **"Not a bone of it will be broken"** (John 19:36, Exodus 12:46) and **"They will look upon him whom they have pierced"** (John 19:37, Numbers 21:9).

Her maternal love was gratified that they would not break the legs of Jesus as they did the two criminals, but her own sword continued to pierce her soul as the soldier's lance opened the side of her Son. Blood and water from the side of Jesus became the universal sign of His divine mercy, and this caused Mary great joy, but only because her submission to the will of Jesus and the Father was so great. Otherwise, such a desecration of the body of Jesus would be unbearable.

This enabled her to receive the lifeless body of her Son and cradle it lovingly in her arms as friends take it carefully down from the cross. The sword of Simeon was now just about tearing out her maternal heart. The most popular iconography of the Sorrowful Mother, the Pieta by Michelangelo, while admirable, can never capture the added pain caused to Mary as she accepted the redeeming body of Jesus and smothered it with tearful kisses.

Finally, Mary knew she must say a final farewell to the flesh of her flesh as some of the braver followers of Jesus guided her to the newly hewn tomb where they hurriedly placed the body of her Son, as the Sabbath time approached. He will now be gone from her. How valiantly she gave in humbly to the realization that her loss will be the gain of all whom Jesus called brothers and sisters—those who believe in what He has done.

A Brief Conversation with Mary

Sweet mother Mary, thank you for this lesson on humility. Teach me how to love to the end. Take me by the hand and relive with me often the tragic moments of the passion and death of your Son. Teach me to be grateful for every single drop of His precious blood that marked the way He trod. Help me to realize that Jesus freely accepted this horrendous deed out of pure love for me. May I humbly accept His gift of blood and water from His side as testimony to the depth of His mercy.

Jesus asked you to be mother again—to me and countless others for whom Jesus gave His life. After all you suffered along with Him, one day the church may officially honor you as Queen of Martyrs, Mediatrix of all graces, and Co-Redemptrix of our good-for-nothing selves.

I have little to offer with you standing at the foot of the cross, Mary, but contempt of self and a great confidence in you with complete self-abandonment to you. I must no longer rely on my own dispositions, intentions, merits, virtues, and good works; I wish to sacrifice them completely to Jesus through you, His loving Mother. I understand that to be why Jesus gave me to you on Calvary. You will make up for my failings and show me to our Lord as His brother.

As you gazed through myriad tears at all the treacheries being performed against the Ruler of the universe hanging in the throes of a willful death, teach me to look up as you did to gain the strength to carry my little crosses.

Help me to live in the will of the Father, as you did, knowing that everything that exists or comes to pass comes ultimately from God. Nothing, trouble or temptation or injury or slander or suffering or punishment or even crucifixion, comes except that the Father wishes me to accept it.

Your early "let it be done to me" at Nazareth has led to a similar one here at the foot of the cross. You joined your fiat to that of your Son as He finished the work of His Father. You show me here that humility is the key to a life of obedience, sacrifice, and love beyond all telling.

O Mary, keep reminding me of how small I really am. Amen.

Mary and the Risen Christ

Although there is no record of the risen Christ appearing to His Blessed Mother, tradition and the writings of many of the fathers of the church teach us that because of His great love and affection for His mother, Jesus must have shared the joy of the resurrection with His most beloved supporter. During the Eastertide, the church prays, "Queen of Heaven, rejoice, for He whom you did merit to bear has risen as He said." Would Jesus forget this and not appear to her? (For a lengthy discussion of this, cf. the author's *The Appearances of the Risen Christ,* IUniverse publishers, 2016).

A special devotion of the Franciscans from at least 1422 has been the Franciscan Crown. This is a seven-decade rosary, honoring the seven joys of Mary, the sixth of which is a reflection of the appearance of Jesus to Mary after His resurrection.

The very fact that there is no mention of this event, especially in the gospel of John, with whom Mary spent many years after the death of Jesus and to whom she revealed much of her hidden life, is testimony again to the humility of Mary. The story of Jesus must be exactly that: the story of Him, not to be muddied with things extraneous to His mission.

Several of the early fathers and doctors of the church held this appearance to be a fact. For one, Ambrose, a church bishop and writer of the fourth century, wrote that Jesus appeared to His mother before He appeared to anyone else (cf. St. Ambrose de Virginit., III, 14, P.L., XVI, 283). This suggests not only that it took place, but also the importance and timing of this meeting.

In the words of Pope Saint John Paul II, delivered in his General Audience on May 21, 1997:

"From this silence, that is, from the fact that the Gospels do not relate an apparition to the Blessed Virgin, one must not deduce that Christ, after his Resurrection, did not appear to Mary... On the contrary, it is legitimate to think that the Mother may really have been the first person to whom the risen Jesus appeared." This clearly is a matter of personal and private devotion, not a formal teaching of the church.

With regard to the profile of the humble Virgin Mary, suffice it to say that according to the teaching of the Messiah, **"The last will be first, and the first will be last"** (Matthew 20:16). Mary's constant posture of humility won for her the first opportunity to rejoice with the glorified Jesus and begin the Alleluia phase of her life. It would be just as hidden, but no more sword. Her humility had triumphed.

If others to whom Jesus appeared were relieved of their anxiety at the death of their master by His permitting them to see Him in His risen state, certainly this was also the case with Mary. However, she probably did not suffer from the same confusion and doubt that troubled them. Her humble submission to the will of the Father, even when that meant suffering through His passion and death alongside Him, brought inner peace. Her joy at seeing Him after His resurrection was one of certitude: a confirmation of her trust that everything would be as He had foretold.

We can imagine the scene, the exact opposite of the sorrowful meeting on the way of the cross.

Perhaps the Blessed Mother was at prayer, confidently waiting for Jesus to rise as He said He would. She addressed herself to her beloved Son, now in the third day of His death: "Come, my beloved, return to us who have faith in You. Gather Your flock together once again, Good Shepherd. Have mercy on the tears of Your afflicted mother, and wash away the sorrow that has engulfed me."

In the midst of these prayers and petitions, her poor little house was suddenly illumined with the light of heaven and the resurrected Son presented Himself to the eyes of His Mother. What a glorious rising of the Son was that first Easter morn. It eclipsed the ball of light rising in the east. She sees only the body of her risen Son, now no longer splattered with blood but glorified as she had dreamed of. He who had smothered her with His loving arms so often in their humble home now extended His arms to her and imprinted the kiss of peace upon her brow. He whom she had lain on the cold slab in the sepulcher was once again burning with the love that only a Son can have for His mother. She thought not of herself and the pain of loss she had been enduring; she thought only of Him and how He had now come into His glory.

Their embrace at this reunion must have been more tender, more mutually fulfilling than any mother-and-son reunion we can imagine. Jesus could see no more of the pain He saw in her look when He glimpsed her at the foot of the cross. Mary need remember the bloodied body she had cradled in her arms after His death only as the means to the glorified body she now beheld.

As he would do with His faithful followers when He appeared to them, Jesus may also have taken a moment to reassure Mary of her role in His new church. She would certainly have a place of honor among His disciples, but she would ask Him to let her remain in the shadows. She would acknowledge that she, like Jesus, had performed her part in God's plan of redemption so that she could now be a moral supporter, but not be in the limelight.

A Brief Conversation with Mary

Sweet mother Mary, thank you for this lesson in humility. I believe you were privileged to witness the risen Christ before all others. I know you deserved this privilege. I respect your continual remaining in the background, even about an event as singular as this. But then how else would I expect you to behave? You who had been chosen in the mind of the Father before all ages to be the one to open the gate of heaven for the Word to become flesh? You never gave in to the temptation to flout your many gifts. You just chose to thank God and praise Him for His goodness. Please teach me to do the same.

My self-love has such a strong hold on me, Mary. How will I ever be able to subdue it as you did? How will I know I am succeeding in this never-ending battle? I recall a story I once heard about getting rid of the last thing holding me back from a perfect love of God.

It had to do with understanding a verse from the last book of the Old Testament: **He will sit refining and purifying silver** (Malachi 3:3). A woman in a Bible study group wondered what this statement meant about the character and nature of God. So she decided to investigate the process of refining silver.

The woman called a silversmith and made an appointment to watch him at work. She didn't mention anything about the reason for her interest beyond her curiosity about the process of refining silver.

As she watched the silversmith, he held a piece of silver over the fire and let it heat up. He explained that in refining silver, one needed to hold the silver in the middle of the fire where the flames were hottest as to burn away all the impurities.

The woman thought about God holding us in such a hot spot, then she thought again about the verse that says: **He will sit refining and purifying silver.** She asked the silversmith if it were true that he had to sit there in front of the fire the whole time the silver was being refined.

The man answered that yes, he not only had to sit there holding the silver but he had to keep his eyes on the silver the entire time it was in the fire. If the silver was left a moment too long in the flames, it would be destroyed.

The woman was silent for a moment. Then she asked the silversmith, "How do you know when the silver is fully refined?" He smiled at her and answered, "Oh, that's easy—when I see my image in it."

I take that to mean, Mary, that I must rework myself until one can see in me the reflection of you and your beloved Son. That is why I try daily to make more perfect my devotion to you, especially in the devout recitation of your Hail Mary and the rosary. St. John Eudes, one of your splendid devotees, is quoted as saying, "I know no surer way of discovering whether a person belongs to God than by finding out if he loves saying the Hail Mary and the rosary."

So help me, Mary, to see the face of God in those I encounter, to see the work of His hand in what I do, so that my big ego is burned out from me.

O Mary, keep reminding me of how small I really am. Amen.

Mary and the Descent of the Spirit

At the beginning of the New Testament text which describes the life of the first Christian community, and after recording the names of the Apostles one by one, Luke states: **All these devoted themselves with**

one accord to prayer, together with some women, and Mary the mother of Jesus, and his brothers** (Acts 1:13). Mary's being the only one mentioned by name must have been out of courtesy and also to indicate the role she had in keeping the little group focused on prayerfully carrying on the work of Jesus. The title of mother, in this context, proclaims the special fostering role that was hers with regard to the early life of her Son's church.

The eleven Apostles were expected to carry out their special command to go into the world and convert all to follow Christ. But they had been told not to do so until the Spirit came to them as a promised gift of the Lord. While awaiting that event, they decided that they needed to fill their number of twelve by selecting a replacement for Judas who had betrayed Jesus. So at one of the meetings when there were some 120 believers present, Peter led the group in choosing someone who had been among the larger group of followers of Jesus from the very beginning. They chose Matthias. There is no mention of Mary having any special influence in this choice, for she did not see it as her prerogative.

But then Luke says, **When the time for Pentecost was fulfilled, they were all in one place together** (Acts 2:1). The word *Pentecost* literally means fiftieth day. So the word does not refer to an event; it simply sets the time for the event. What event? What is then described by Luke in verses 2–4 is the miraculous descent of the Holy Spirit upon the group and their initial reaction. Writing about it later, Luke chose the time to stand for the occurrence, which has been carried down to the present time.

Just about every painting or picture of Pentecost shows Mary alongside the Apostles with fiery tongues over their heads, indicating that tradition teaches that Mary was there to receive this new indwelling of the Spirit. She, of course, had been overshadowed by that same Spirit as Jesus was conceived of Him. As a result, it is believed by most that she had already received all the gifts and fruits and virtues that come from the third person of the Trinity. Nonetheless, since Mary was an integral and active participant in the early life of the church, it seems appropriate that she would receive this extra gift that her Son had promised to His close associates. Otherwise, she would have had to do the impossible by saying, "Skip me, Holy Spirit, because You already came down upon me!"

Furthermore, since this day is considered the birthday of the church, it was essential that Mary, the mother of the church, would be present for this infusion of the Spirit.

The first reaction of those being so gifted, according to the Acts 1:4, was for them to speak in tongues. Verses 7 to 8 explain further that this meant that the speech of Galileans was heard in the native tongues of many devout Jews who were gathered in Jerusalem at the time. Was Mary one of those so speaking? Maybe, but if so, then she too would have been the butt of some present who scoffed that **"They have had too much new wine"** (Acts 1:13). Mary could accept that too, for on at least one occasion, even Jesus was demeaned by his own family: **"he is out of his mind"** (Mark 3:21). She could accept that and more in her spirit of humility.

The post-Pentecost years were a continuation of the community living begun while awaiting the promised Spirit. When Pope Saint John Paul II called Mary "Woman of the Eucharist" (cf. Ecclesia de Eucharistia, April 17, 22003, #53), he said, "Mary must have continued to be present at the Eucharistic celebrations of the first generation of Christians, who were devoted to the breaking of the bread" (Acts 2:42). In keeping with the command of Jesus, **"do this in memory of me"** (Luke 22:19), the Apostles made this the center of their frequent gatherings, and Mary was right there with them, humbly acknowledging that they had a gift not granted to her.

Servant of God Jean Claude Colin, founder of the Society of Mary, or the Marists, offered the community action and spirit of the early Christians as a model for the religious community named after Mary. He suggested these first followers of Christ were ordinary men and women who gathered for prayer and the Eucharist, and then, being transformed by the gospel story, they would return to the world so as in turn to transform it after the image of Jesus.

A Brief Conversation with Mary

Sweet mother Mary, thank you for this lesson in humility. There were so many things you taught us by your participation in the early life of the church. Pope Saint John Paul II described you as being "imbued with charity and a witness of faith." He saw you "passing on your recollection of the incarnation, the hidden life, and the mission of Jesus as you sought to strengthen the belief of the others." In the absence of further details in scripture, he assures us that your post-Pentecost life "would have continued to be hidden and discreet, watchful and effective." You deeply influenced the community of the Lord's disciples (cf. Pope John Paul II, General Audience, May 28, 1997).

    I have told you often that I wish to honor you by imitating your virtues, especially your humility. I can assume you also want me to try to be the same kind of helpful influence on those around me. Just as you saw to it that the seeds of the Spirit planted in you bore much fruit, so am I to cultivate the seeds the Spirit given to me in baptism and confirmation so that they blossom as virtues for the good of my surroundings. May I have the courage to do this in a quiet way.

    I just used the word *wish* to honor you or *wish* to develop the virtue of humility. That was a slip of the tongue. I learned a long time ago that there is a difference between wishing something and willing it.

If I *wish* to be humble, that simply means I hope to possess that virtue but then make excuses along the way for failing to do so. If I *will* it, I will brook no excuses; I will apply my every act of willpower to be humble, focusing not only on the desired end but also on the means to obtain it. That's how important it must be for me to live your hidden life.

Your challenge at this time was to guide the infant church to holiness in adhering to the precepts of your beloved Son. We Christians in each age have had the same duty: to give witness to the teachings of Jesus in our words but even more so in our actions. As the hymn says, "They will know we are Christians by our love." As you did for the despondent Apostles waiting for the Holy Spirit, so I am called to comfort others in their discouragements, support them in their weariness, raise them up when they fall, applaud their successes. Help me to show them your Son, our God and our all. That will help me to think less of myself.

I understand that this does not mean I have to look for opportunities to be of service to others in some unusual manner. Rather, I believe it means just proceeding with the everyday events of my life. Opportunities will present themselves, if I really have my eyes and ears open for them. Otherwise, I will be putting myself in the limelight, rather than imitating you in your hidden life, hidden in the daily chores of living the life God grants to me.

Such actions will come if I am predisposed for them. Such a readiness can come if I am aloof from the cares of this world and acquire the virtue of recollection. One of the so-called habits of any practicing Catholic is said to be contemplation, which is nothing but a continual sense of the presence of God, as was a mark of your life. One author even equates a hidden life with a life of prayer (cf. *The Hidden Life of Prayer*, The Life Blood of the Christian, by David McIntyre, Christian Heritage, November 20, 2010).

As you received the gifts of the Holy Spirit, one we especially note when we address you as the Seat of Wisdom. I have no need of modern-day gurus; you point me to the fount of the knowledge of good and evil. May I turn always to the Holy Spirit and repeat your words: "How can this be?" Help me, I pray, to always choose right not wrong, life not death.

O Mary, keep reminding me of how small I really am. Amen.

The Assumption of Mary

Mary lived her humble life in the early church for some years under the careful protection of St. John into whose care she had been entrusted by Jesus on Calvary. St. Antoninus of Florence wondered if Mary visited the places where her Son had done any miraculous deed and there contemplate the sacred mysteries. Did she go to Nazareth, to the place where the angel had made his announcement to her and she had conceived the Son of God, and there contemplate God's boundless charity? Did she visit Bethlehem and meditate on God's humility, for there He had His humble birth? Did she go to the temple in Jerusalem, where she had been presented on the fortieth day and where her Son later preached, recalling His most sweet and wondrous teaching, reflecting on His wisdom? Did she visit the river Jordan, where when Christ was baptized He had made all the waters holy for washing away the sins of those receiving baptism and where John had heard the Father's voice: "This is my beloved Son," and the Holy Spirit was seen in the likeness of a dove? Passing by Mt. Calvary, where her Son was crucified amid such great insults for the salvation of men, was she completely dissolved into tears because of the immense sweetness of God's love that was revealed there? And going up to the Mount of Olives, did she recall that her Son had ascended from there into heaven, and eagerly longed to be with Christ?

So hidden was her post-resurrection life that no one knows exactly when she passed from this life to her eternal reward in heaven. There is one tradition that has come down from at least since the fifth century that Mary died between three and fifteen years after the ascension of Jesus into heaven.

Since the Middle Ages, another view prevailed that she died of love, her great desire to be united to her Son either dissolving the ties of body and soul, or prevailing on God to dissolve them. Her passing away is a sacrifice of love, completing the dolorous sacrifice of her life.

St. Juvenal, bishop of Jerusalem, asserted at the Council of Chalcedon in 351 that Mary had died in the presence of the Apostles. Another story that gained much credence stated that one of the Apostles, often identified as St. Thomas, was not present at the death of Mary but his late arrival precipitated a reopening of Mary's tomb, which was found to be empty except for her grave clothes. Because of this, reportedly the Apostles assumed Mary had been bodily assumed into heaven, much as her Son had.

Suffice it to say that from earliest times, Christians believed that one of Mary's gifts, associated with her being conceived without original sin or any of its unhappy consequences, like death, was to be taken up into heaven after the completion of her earthly life. It was called Mary's Assumption or her dormition.

This became a dogma of the Catholic church in 1950. "Considerations of the holy fathers, based on sacred writings, see the loving mother of God as most intimately joined to her divine Son as always sharing his lot . . . Hence . . . she finally obtained . . . that she should be preserved from the corruption of the tomb, and taken up body and soul to the glory of heaven" (apostolic constitution *Munificentissimus Deus*, Pope Pius XII, November 1, 1950).

With regard to sacred scripture, the pope referred to Genesis, chapter 3, verse 15, alluding to Mary's victory over sin and death. He then traced Christian belief in this privilege of Mary through the teaching of the early fathers of the church, down through the middle ages and to his own time. Referring also to the more recent declaration of the Immaculate Conception (1854), Pope Pius gloried in the development of these doctrines concerning Mary in our modern age and then declared the Assumption to be a matter of faith.

By stressing the togetherness of Jesus and Mary, Pope Pius reaffirmed the church's belief in Mary as the noble associate of the divine Redeemer. He taught us that just as Jesus won a complete triumph over sin and death by His resurrection, so Mary completed her triumph over sin and death by her assumption into heaven, body and soul.

Some have argued that if this is such an important teaching that it deserved to be defined by the infallibility of the pope, why did it take almost two millennia to be so recognized?

Jesus Himself was careful not to try to teach His followers everything, in recognition of the ability of the human mind to comprehend only so much at a time. **"I have much more to tell you, but you cannot bear it now"** (John 16:12). It was most important that the church solidify its dogmatic teachings about Jesus, the Trinity, and other important articles of faith revolving around the deity in the first few centuries. Those dealing with Mary's maternity and virginity were defined early because they involved Jesus. Only later did the church deem it time to define her Immaculate Conception (1854) and assumption (1950).

We can see Mary's humility concurring with this sequence of events. Even Dante described Mary as "high beyond all others, lowlier than none" (cf. Paradise XXXIII, 3). Truly Mary's gifts showed the height of her place in the eyes of God, while taking the last place in the order of being honored publicly.

Is that the end of the story about Mary? Hardly. From her lofty position at the right hand of her Son, Mary is ever our mother, caring for all of us as she had been instructed to do by Jesus when He gave us all to her on Calvary. She continues to plead our cause before the throne of God. She is our advocate, our mediator. She is the dispenser of all graces from her Son.

In the final analysis it is she on whom we pin our hopes and prayers for a final disposition of God's mercy, as we keep reminding her when we recite her favorite prayer: "Holy Mary, Mother of God, pray for us sinners now, and at the hour of our death. Amen."

Pope Leo XIII wrote, "It may be affirmed that, according to God's will, nothing comes to us without going through Mary's hands. Just as no one can approach the Almighty Father except through the Son, so no one can approach Christ except through his Mother" (Encyclical: *Octobri Mense,* September 22, 1891). After Jesus, who is the only Mediator, Mary is the mediatrix; as Jesus continually intercedes with the Father in heaven on our behalf, so Mary intercedes with Jesus for us. She obtains and dispenses to us all the graces we need.

Shortly later Pope Saint Pius X explained further: "By the communion of sorrows and of will between Christ and Mary, she merited to become the dispenser of all the benefits which Jesus acquired for us by shedding his Blood" (Encyclical: *Ad Diem Illum,* February 2, 1904). Mary, who was associated in the closest and most intimate way with the life, the work, and the passion of her Son, cooperated with Him in our redemption to such an extent that she is venerated by many as our Co-Redemptrix. What Jesus merited for us directly, Mary won for us through her association with her Son. Thus Mary obtained real power over all the supernatural treasures acquired by her Son, and since she obtained them together with Him, she also distributes them to us with Him.

A Brief Conversation with Mary

Sweet mother Mary, thank you for this lesson in humility. How happy I am to add my voice to the chorus of praise that continues to honor you. As we learn to recognize the tremendous glory with which you are loved by God Himself and identify the special honors He bestows on you, we thank God for this special recognition He gives to you. We appreciate that these more recent pontifical declarations are not something the church has invented, nor do they take away anything from the honor and glory due to God alone. They are just further clarifications of all that was implied in those verses of scripture which we call your Magnificat. It was, after all, the Spirit speaking through you when you said, **"For he has looked upon his handmaid's lowliness; behold, from now on all ages will call me blessed. The Mighty One has done great things for me"** (Luke 1:48–9).

Thank you for helping us to continue to learn all those great things He has done for you.

I do not find it difficult at all to honor you and recite your blessings. Like a loving son that I wish to be, I take pride in the recognition given you by our Father in heaven. By contemplating these gifts, I recognize them as awards for your great humility. I am only one poor soul among all the generations which you foretold would call you blessed because of your dutiful submission to the will of God. Just as Jesus honored you by this singular gift, I commit myself to honoring you. In honoring you, I give testimony to the goodness and mercy of our Father.

Assumed into heaven, you still remain the mother given to me by Jesus. I therefore try to make myself like unto you as children should resemble their mother. Consequently, I endeavor to imitate your patience, your obedience, your purity, your mildness and docility, your charity, and especially your humility. I beseech you, gentle mother in heaven, to look upon me, your unworthy child, to protect and to guide me in all things and to be a mother to me both in life and in death.

How often Jesus held up for our edification the humility of a child, warning that we must be like children to enter the gates of heaven. As you look down on me from that hoped-for destiny of mine, I look up with the trust of such a child. How easy it is to put myself in your loving hand, knowing that you will never let go. If ever a child could trust its mother for loving care, I am confident that you will reward my child-like trust with the motherly care Jesus bids you give to me.

I have been trying to learn how to imitate your humility. I know how strong my tendency to self-love and its consequent selfishness is. As I gaze on a painting of your glorious ascension into the arms of your Son, I feel no need to mouth words. I have only to gaze upon you. With eyes fixed on your beauty, with admiration for your happiness, with envy for the ministering angels who fly to your embrace, with joy in my heart for your exaltation, with thanksgiving for your return look of motherly love, I simply rejoice in joining in the hymns of Alleluia which accompany you to your place at the right hand of Jesus. I see the peace and self-fulfillment that is yours because of your life of following the will of our Father. I wish the same for myself.

St. Alphonsus Liguori taught that God looks with a benevolent eye on all who love Mary. Besides

His own glory, God desires nothing more than to see her honored and loved by all. From you, O Mary, I hope for every grace. I look to you to obtain the forgiveness of all my sins and the gift of perseverance. I pray always that you assist me in the hour of my death, to rescue me from purgatory, and finally to welcome me into heaven.

As I call upon you to remember your promise to help me get through the pearly gates, I am reminded of the caution given by our Lord when He reminded us that the gate is a narrow one. I understand that to mean that one who is puffed up with himself will not be able to pass through. I must follow your example and be small and unencumbered with all the baggage I have accumulated. Only those who humble themselves before God and fellow man will fit.

O Mary, keep reminding me of how small I really am. Amen.

The Coronation of Mary as Queen

In defining the Assumption as a dogma of our faith, Pope Pius XII went on to say, "She might be taken up body and soul to the glory of heaven, where, as queen, she sits in splendor at the right hand of her

Son, the immortal King of the Ages" (Apostolic constitution Munificentissimus Deus, #42, November 1, 1950). Less than two decades later, the Vatican Council II taught: "Finally, preserved from all guilt of original sin, the Immaculate Virgin was taken up body and soul into heavenly glory upon the completion of her earthly sojourn. She was exalted by the Lord as Queen of all" (Lumen Gentium #59).

Though it is not clear that the queenship is an article of faith, the addition of that last sentence in each of these quotations suggests that Mary, after being assumed into heaven, was afforded another special privilege. She was enthroned as queen of heaven and earth. The church has established two separate feasts to commemorate each of these gifts: the Assumption of Mary and the Coronation of Mary as Queen of the Universe.

If ever there was a realization of the teaching of Jesus that the last shall be first (Matthew 25:12), it has been evidenced by the transition of the humble handmaid of the Lord to the virgin queen of all. **Humble yourselves before the Lord and he will exalt you** (James 4:10). Yet even now in her exalted state, the entrenched virtue of humility continues to shine forth in Mary as she remains closely united to her Son for all eternity, her immaculate heart reigning next to the sacred heart of Jesus.

St. John gave us this description of this queen: **A great sign appeared in the sky, a woman clothed with the sun, with the moon under her feet, and on her head a crown of twelve stars** (Revelation

12:1). At the end times, this queen will have special duties in aiding her Son to sort the sheep from the goats. Meanwhile, in keeping with her comfort in being humble, Mary, in such a place of power at the throne of God, remains hidden, working behind the scenes in our behalf. She constantly encourages us to accept the will of God as she did. She is our advocate, our mediatrix, presenting our requests to Jesus, begging Him to satisfy our needs, even before we mention them.

The moon under Mary's feet is the symbol of death, mortality and all transitory things, of all that has been overcome by the passion of Jesus and Mary's own sorrowful sacrifices. Mary has triumphed over them. Yet as the loving mother that she remains, she cannot forget us and our weaknesses. She prays for us, sinners, anxious to usher us into the Promised Land. She accepts her regal role as one of begging still, for coronation notwithstanding, she knows her place vis-a-vis her Son and our heavenly Father.

It is difficult to keep the right balance between Mary's exaltation and her submission or what is called her hidden life and humility. Mary's own hymn, the Magnificat, gives perfect expression to both. She is still now, as she was then, the handmaid of the Lord, but a handmaid to whom He has done great things, hence all generations call her blessed. She is handmaid because no creature can be more in relation to the sovereign majesty of God. But this same God has done such great things in her and has given her so many graces, because He made her the mother of His only co-equal Son. Who are we, then, to confer any less dignity and honor to her, while acknowledging her own preference to be considered a handmaid?

Vatican II speaks clearly about our ability to give whatever honor we deem appropriate to Mary, when it says: "The synod does not have it in mind to give a complete doctrine on Mary, nor does it wish to decide those questions which have not yet been fully illuminated by the work of theologians. Those opinions therefore may be lawfully retained which are fully propounded by schools of Catholic thought concerning her who occupies a place in the church which is the highest after Christ and yet very close to us" (Lumen Gentium #54).

Another picture of Mary, queen of heaven, was shown to St. Bridget of Sweden, during one of her many apparitions to this saint. Mary described herself as being, as it were, a gardener of the world. When a human gardener sees the rise of strong wind harmful to the little plants and the trees of his garden, he hastens to bind them fast with sturdy stakes so that they not be broken by the rushing wind or even uprooted. Mary lovingly portrayed her role as queen as doing the same in the garden of this world. When she sees the dangerous winds of the devil's temptations and wicked suggestions attacking the hearts of human beings, she at once has recourse to the Lord, helping her children with her prayers and obtaining from Jesus infusions of the Holy Spirit to prop them up to keep them spiritually uninjured by the diabolic winds.

A Brief Conversation with Mary

Sweet mother Mary, thank you for this lesson in humility. The church has long recognized you as the woman described by St. John in the book of Revelation. Adorned with the sun as a shining light, as queen of the universe, you do not glory in your exalted position; instead, you use this shining light as the Stella Maris, or Star of the Sea, as a guide for us. Even as queen, you do not boast of your accomplishments, as rewarded by Jesus. Teach me to boast of your love for us rather than my accomplishments.

As the mother of God, you had to become the mother of the church of your Son, and so you continue to be, reigning next to the Sacred Heart of Jesus. It was your unconditional yes to the archangel that empowered you to be the mother of Jesus and our mother too and earned for you the place beside Him which you now enjoy. Teach me, I pray, to say yes without reservations to the Lord's will. It's that unconditional part that is scary. The easy demands of the Lord are met with an easy compliance. It's the commands that are resisted by my powerful ego that cause the problem. Such has been the course of my life, for I have learned all too late that yes means accepting everything.

I must learn to say no at times: no to seeking power, money, pleasure, dishonesty, complicity, hypocrisy, corruption, and all other kinds of selfishness. As your foot crushes the head of the serpent, help me to say a crushing no to all these things. Help me, Mother Mary, to see that to be beside you in heaven means to be beside you in surrendering my will in all things. Enlighten me, from your place on high, to distinguish the good from the bad, what I should welcome from what I should shun.

As you continue to be an example for us, as you unceasingly intercede for us, you suggest that I do my part. One way of doing this, as I contemplate your queenship is to pay less attention to the things of this world, represented by the moon under your feet, and to think of the things above, not those of the earth (Colossians 3:2).

I ask you to accept me as one of your faithful servants, oh, queen mother! I wish to give myself to you as one of your subjects, promising to serve and honor you in all my life in every way possible. This is not to lessen my servitude to your Son but to add a measure of honor to you as well. I remember the motto of the Marist fathers who played a large part in my formation of serving you: "For the Greater Glory of God, *and the honor of the mother of God.*" Oh, that I could always remember to serve you, to praise you, to honor you, and make you loved by everybody!

I contemplate your entire life of surrender to the will of the Father, from that first fiat to the ultimate sacrifice of your Son on the cross and even to the way you spend eternity begging for mercy on the likes of us. It's as though you say, "My life has been one of giving myself to the work God has in mind for me, and I cannot stop doing the same even in heaven." I do not deserve your special attention, but I get it anyway. You teach me that it is love that wins out in the end. Blessed are you among women!

It is a peaceful submitting to the will of God that earns the crown when the battle is over. Teach me, Queen of Peace; continue to guide me in your school of humility. I put myself entirely in your hands as the surest way of pleasing Jesus. By doing so, I imitate God the Father, who gave us His Son only through you and who imparts His graces to us only through you.

O Mary, keep reminding me of how small I really am. Amen.

To love Mary and to make her loved!

About the Author

After spending five years as a professed religious in the Society of Mary (the Marists), Doctor Deegan enjoyed a successful career as a strategic planner for corporations and religious organizations. Now retired, his recent books include *Bread of Life Discourse*, a meditation on chapter 6 of St. John's gospel, and *The Appearances of the Risen Christ*, an examination of twelve times Jesus appeared before His ascension. As a Bible study leader, he tries to help readers mine new insights from oft-read passages of the Bible. He, his wife, and family reside in Florida.

www.ingramcontent.com/pod-product-compliance
Lightning Source LLC
LaVergne TN
LVHW040150080526
838202LV00042B/3102